Japan's
Multinational
Enterprises

Japan's Multinational Enterprises

M. Y. Yoshino

Harvard University Press
Cambridge, Massachusetts
and London, England
1976

Library of Congress Cataloging in Publication Data

Yoshino, Michael Y
  Japan's multinational enterprises.

  Includes index.
  1. Corporations, Japanese. 2. International
business enterprises. I. Title.
HD2907.Y63   338.8'8'0952   76-26602
ISBN 0-674-47259-4

To Raymond Vernon

Acknowledgments

This book was prepared as part of the Harvard Multinational Enterprise project. I owe a special debt of gratitude to Professor Raymond Vernon, the director of the project. Only Mr. Vernon and I know the extent to which he so generously gave his ideas. The financial support of the study came mainly from the Ford Foundation, whose generosity I gratefully acknowledge.

Most of the data for the book were obtained from executives of Japanese enterprises. Throughout the field study, I had the pleasure of interviewing scores of managers both in Japan and abroad. Without exception they generously shared their experiences with me. I wish to make a general statement of appreciation for the full cooperation of my respondents. Although the great majority of my respondents must remain anonymous, I would like to express my gratitude to the following individuals who provided invaluable introductions to a number of companies: Yoshizane Iwasa, Chairman of the Board of the Fuji Bank; Shigeki Tashiro, Honorary Chairman of the Board of Toray, Inc.; Sohei Nakayama, Advisor to the Industrial Bank of Japan; Wataru Tajitsu, Chairman of the Board of the Mitsubishi Bank; Kazue Kitagawa, former Chairman of the Board of Sumitomo Electric Company; Mr. Mionoru Abe, formerly Executive Vice President of Teijin Inc., now President of Teijin Seiki Ltd.

I am also thankful to Max Hall, a colleague and friend who read the manuscript and gave me many insights.

Finally, I would like to acknowledge my gratitude to my wife and children who together provided invaluable support to this undertaking.

Contents

Tables

Introduction

by Raymond Vernon

Over ten years ago, a number of scholars at the Harvard Business School began to link up in a joint research effort that eventually came to be called the Harvard Multinational Enterprise Project. What tied us together was a common interest in studying the multinational spread of big enterprises. Some were interested in the techniques, strategies, and structures of these enterprises, some in the economic consequences of their operations, some in even larger questions. That work has gone on ever since, fueled mainly by several generous grants from the Ford Foundation, and it has produced a steady output of books, articles, theses, and data banks.

Necessarily, we devoted a good deal of our early work to measurement and description; but it was measurement and description of a specialized kind. Since our professional skills lay mainly in understanding the multinational enterprise as an economic institution—an institution for the making and selling of goods and services—we stressed that side of its existence, leaving the fascinating and important questions of political and social aspects mainly to others. Even with that orientation, however, there were plenty of contentious issues to be explored and plenty of processes to be understood.

For instance, there were those who insisted that the multinational spread of business was nothing new or exciting—that it went back to the Italian city states and the British East India Company. And there were those who contended that it had all begun yesterday and was in process of engulfing the world's economies. Some were convinced that the motivations and strategies of the multinationalizing firms were pretty much the same as those of any large firm, even those that stayed at home; some were of the view that the multinationalizing trend represented something very new. Some thought that, in economic terms, the trend was good for the home countries of the enterprises and bad for the countries into which they had spread; some thought that the good and bad should be stated in reverse. As questions such as these became more and more politicized throughout the 1960s and 1970s, opinions tended to increase rather more rapidly than the facts.

From the very beginnings of the project, those who participated were confronted with one difficult problem. We could not be sure to what extent the motives, methods, and effects of multinational spread were affected by the home nationality of the enterprises involved. How much weight was to be attributed to the fact that Nestle's home was in Switzerland, that Phillips was Dutch, IBM American, and Matsushita Japanese?

We dealt with that uncertainty by taking the conservative approach. For years, we ostentatiously couched our hypotheses and framed our studies solely in terms of the U.S.-based enterprise. Our first series of publications was explicitly limited in this way. These included my own book, *Sovereignty at Bay* (1971); one by S. M. Robbins and R. B. Stobaugh, *Money in the Multinational Enterprise* (1973); a third by J. M. Stopford and L. T. Wells, *Managing the Multinational Enterprise* (1972); and several dozen articles and monographs.

However, there was no holding down the desire of the group to explore the phenomenon for enterprises based in other countries. Some of the group's hypotheses about the U.S.-based enterprises demanded such comparative studies. For instance, if the multinationalizing trend had something to do with innovation, as the U.S. data seemed to indicate, what should one expect of enterprises that were based in countries where very little innovation occurred? If other conditions of the home market figured in various hypotheses about multinational spread, could the hypotheses not be better tested by the comparative approach?

And what of organizational adaptations to the multinational strategy? Did the adaptations of a Ford or a General Electric represent a universal phenomenon, unrelated to the home culture; or should one expect a different pattern from Nissan and Sony?

The special problems that bedevil comparative research are all too well known. Any observer has an angle of cultural vision. And a U.S.-trained, U.S.-based observer, let loose among the enterprises of Britain, Germany, and Japan, could easily be a threat to his subject and himself. On the other hand, if a British researcher were charged with researching Britain, an Italian researcher with researching Italy, and a Japanese researcher with doing Japan, other risks were entailed. For example, a comparative approach organized in this way might be less than ideal for testing unifying and synthesizing hypotheses which related the various country groups to one another.

Luck was with us. In 1969, at the moment when we had to make a choice of research strategy, Michael Yoshino invited us to collaborate with him in his own exploration of the multinational spread of Japan-based enterprises.

Having been present at the creation, I must at all costs be guarded in my expressions of enthusiasm for Yoshino's work. But restraint is a virtue only up to a point.

Yoshino is a rare researcher: born and raised in Japan, educated partly in Japanese schools, partly in the United States; an academic in the United States, yet one whose books on Japanese enterprises are acknowledged as authoritative by scholars in both countries. So we seized the opportunity of the proffered partnership, thereby acquiring in one transaction a collaborator, a colleague, and a friend.

Under Yoshino's pen, the Japanese version of the multinationalizing trend in business becomes familiar, plausible, and intellectually manageable. Many of the hypotheses that were articulated in the U.S. stage of the study manage to survive, even to gain strength; but almost always the hypotheses, having been elaborated in another dimension, are enriched beyond their original form.

At the same time, the quintessential Japanese elements of the multinationalizing process are isolated and analyzed, in ways that can only be done by someone completely familiar with Japanese society. The Japanese elements of the process emerge, identified and analyzed, and they prove no more occult than the more familiar U.S. variants.

Japan, it can be assumed, will have a major place in the world economy over the next few decades. Like any other large nation, its increased importance will create major risks and generate major opportunities both for itself and for others. The process of spread in which Japanese business is engaged needs to be well understood—understood not only by other countries but also by Japan itself. Yoshino's work represents a large contribution to that critical objective.

1. The Setting

By the early 1970s it became increasingly apparent that Japanese industrial enterprises had committed themselves to a new strategy—a strategy of foreign direct investment. Japanese copper mining in Zaire, oil drilling in Saudi Arabia, textile plants in Thailand, television factories in the United States, automobile assembly in Mexico, shipbuilding in Brazil—all attest to the growing multinational presence of Japanese industries. The commitment to foreign manufacturing and resource development under foreign control represents a major shift from the earlier strategy of export. During the last hundred years, Japanese enterprises had relentlessly and successfully penetrated the world market by means of trade.

Initially, exports consisted of a variety of simple foodstuffs and industrial raw materials. Among them were tea, dried fish, copper, gold and coal from newly developed mines, and wood and straw products. By far the most important throughout the decades of the 1870s, 80s, and 90s was silk. By the turn of the century, the new cotton industry was firmly established and cotton textile products dominated Japanese export. Though textile continued to be the main export throughout these prewar decades, by the early 1930s Japanese exports included substantial amounts of metal goods and machineries, processed foods, and even chemicals and drugs.

After World War II, Japanese enterprises turned even more to the export market, this time with products of capital-intensive and skill-intensive industries. By the mid-1960s they had built a commanding global position in export products like giant tankers, steel, automobiles, and transistor radios.

In the light of the historic success of the export strategy, several questions can be raised. Why did the change in strategy

1

come about? What are the chief elements in the newly emerging strategy? Has the new strategy led to realignment of the existing system of management in Japanese firms?

The dynamic interaction of environment, strategy, and structure has been analyzed by Alfred Chandler in a study of the evolution of the most successful American enterprises. Chandler identified common elements pertaining to the process of change in a large number of companies in different industries. These companies were led by innovative executives who perceived new threats and opportunities in the changing environment and sought to establish new strategies to fend off the threats and capitalize on the opportunities. But the pursuit of a new strategy often required the creation of a new structure.[1]

Although no exhaustive or systematic analysis has yet been made of Japan's major enterprises, a close look at their history during the past century reveals that they too undertook a series of changes in strategy and structure—first during the several decades of rapid industrialization prior to 1945, then again in their post-World War II resurgence. Yet until recently almost all the changes in both strategy and structure had taken place at home. Indeed, commitment to multinational strategy would have special implications for Japanese enterprises. The environment in Japan is highly homogeneous. The society is cohesive and well integrated. The social, educational, and even ideological backgrounds of the men who work in large enterprises are very similar. Managerial practices and the system of employment have further reinforced the homogenization of the managerial cadres. Therefore, to implement a strategy of multinationalization, Japanese managers have been compelled to bridge great physical distances, and more important, to accommodate themselves to different social and cultural values.

The research upon which this book is based had the purpose of understanding the process by which Japanese enterprises evolved their multinational strategies and of pinpointing the structural changes made in response to them. I also wish to identify and account for the similarities and differences between the patterns characteristic of the multinational enterprises of Japan and the patterns of other nations, particularly the United States. The first main step is to identify major changes in the environment—changes that prompted Japan's leading enterprises to pursue a strategy of multinationalization. And this requires a brief historical analysis of the strategy formulation and structural responses of Japanese enterprises during the event-packed century from 1868 to 1970.

Strategy and Structure, 1868–1945

The industrialization of Japan dates back to 1868, the year of the Meiji Restoration, when a small group of young men of lower warrior class overthrew the decaying Tokugawa feudal system that had ruled Japan for the previous two and a half centuries. There were two distinct aspects of the movement that are relevant here. One was the fact that the Meiji Restoration was not a popular revolt—a mass uprising against the ruling elite. Remarkable and thorough as it was, the Restoration was actually imposed by members of the ruling elite. The other is that the immediate impetus for the Restoration came in the form of a foreign military threat. A strong commitment to the mercantile policy of the era had pushed European countries and the United States into Asia, and by the 1860s Japan was one of the few countries in East Asia yet to be conquered. In the light of this threat, the young elite which had come to power felt that their first priority was to build sufficient military strength to assure Japan's political independence.[2] Brief but dramatic encounters with the advanced weapons of the Western nations had convinced them that industrialization was a prerequisite to modern military strength. Thus, when the Japanese elite turned vigorously to programs of industrialization, their objective was clear and so were their national priorities.[3]

The new government took the initiative in starting modern industries not for profound ideological reasons but out of sheer pragmatism. The merchant class, thrust into the rather chaotic political and economic environment of the era and totally lacking prior experience in manufacturing, was reluctant to undertake new industrial ventures. To defend their coasts against foreign invasions and to enhance their revenue, a few progressive clans within the Tokugawa feudal system had started modern industries prior to the Restoration. Over these enterprises, the clan governments had maintained direct control. Since most of the Meiji leadership came from these clans, they were not totally unfamiliar with the idea of government leadership in industry. The new regime took over the modern enterprises started by the progressive clans and pioneered in developing railroads, communication facilities, mining, shipbuilding, and military arsenals.[4] It also pressed for social and political reforms. In promoting modernization, it turned to the West for technology as well as for institutional frameworks.

The Meiji leaders quickly saw the importance of export. They needed exports to pay for the purchase of modern weapons and machineries, to hire foreign advisers, and to send Japanese abroad for training. In the immediate aftermath of the Meiji Restoration, a brief period of exploitation by the few foreign agents quickly taught the Japanese that foreign trade requires specialized technical knowledge, familiarity with market conditions, and financial resources.

The national need to develop exports, together with the fresh opportunities opening up after two centuries of self-imposed isolation, soon led to the formation of the so-called trading companies. In 1872, with active encouragement from the government, Mitsui, which had been a successful merchant family for nearly two centuries prior to the Restoration, became the first to establish such an organization. Mitsubishi soon followed suit. These struggling new companies engaged in the export of a few items such as tea, rice, and raw silk. For the first decade or so, they were not much different from the earlier British version of trading companies and performed only the rudimentary functions of foreign trade. It is not until the trading company became an integral part of Zaibatsu that it took on unique characteristics.

In 1880 the Japanese government took an important step, one that was to shape the subsequent pattern of Japan's industrial development: it decided to dispose of most of the enterprises it had initiated. Its reasons, once again, were pragmatic.[5] By that time government leaders had become preoccupied with political and social reforms. They were also feeling a need to make broad economic policies rather than to initiate and manage specific industries and individual enterprises. Moreover, profits from the enterprises proved to be meager and the government needed funds for armament. Furthermore, by this time, a small number of entrepreneurs, close to the ruling oligarchy, had emerged, and they could serve as a national instrument in the further development of Japanese industries. Some of these men and families, like Mitsui, had amassed considerable wealth prior to the Restoration; others achieved eminence in the chaotic era of the Meiji Restoration. In fact, some of them had helped finance the Restoration movement. Some, like Koyata Iwasaki, the founder of Mitsubishi, were active participants in the movement itself.

These new entrepreneurs had much in common with the ruling oligarchy. They came from a similar social background and shared a peculiar Meiji ideology, which combined patriotism, nationalism, and personal ambition.[6] By favoring this particular group of entrepreneurs, the ruling elite was assured that they could continue to exert their influence over the course of the nation's industrial development. The government enterprises were sold at bargain prices, and the families that purchased them took on a central role in developing Japan's modern industries.

The strategy for industrialization that Japan set out to pursue in the 1880s had many familiar elements. For key industries, the government provided heavy subsidies and protection against import. It vigorously promoted export in order to pay for the import of technology, machinery, and raw materials. Export revenue was also important to finance the development of Japan's infrastructure and to bolster her military strength. In the pursuit of this strategy, Japan faced a set of problems commonly encountered by developing countries—shortage of capital, technology, and managerial talents. Japan's struggling industries developed a unique institution.

Even after the government sold its own enterprises, the ruling elite continued to turn to a handful of prominent families for initiating new industrial and financial undertakings. After all, only a few families possessed sufficient capital and technical resources to do so. In return, the government showered them with patronage ranging from generous government contracts to liberal subsidies. High government officials served as advisers to these families, who in turn rewarded them handsomely. These families evolved gradually into a unique Japanese economic institution known as *Zaibatsu*.[7] The Zaibatsu, as it developed, became a group of giant diversified companies under the control of a family-owned holding company. Included in the group were banks, insurance companies, trading companies, shipping firms, and a host of manufacturing enterprises. Among a dozen or so Zaibatsu which came into being, four were particularly prominent. They were Mitsui, Mitsubishi, Sumitomo, and Yasuda.

The Zaibatsu's uniqueness lay in its distinct structure, which ingeniously combined Western concepts of corporation and Japan's traditional values. Zaibatsu borrowed the Western concept of a joint stock company, a radical notion for the Japanese in the 1880s and adopted every means of corporate control familiar in the West. The holding company extended through a network of subsidiaries and affiliates, intercorporate stockholding, interlocking directorates, management agreements, and bank credit. Through ingenious combinations of these means, the holding company controlled a large number of subsidiaries, affiliates, and subcontractors. Day-to-day decisions were made by the heads of the units, but all key decisions, particularly those affecting the entire group, were made by the holding company itself.

Just as basic an instrument of central control as the Western forms of organization were the traditional Japanese values that emphasized hierarchical relationships, Confucian-based authoritarianism, the importance of the collectivity, and discipline. In structuring its administrative system, the Zaibatsu drew heavily on the distinctive Japanese concept of family. Traditionally, the family in Japan was far more than a biological kinship group.[8] It was a network of related households, all of whose members were subject to the authority of a single head, and it was also the primary framework for structuring all types of secondary groups. In fact, the family emerged as a collective organization much broader in its significance and composition than a purely biological unit. Thus, to the Japanese, the hierarchical arrangement of subsidiaries and affiliated companies under the helm of a holding company took on a special meaning.

Moreover, the traditional concept of family, which extended beyond a kinship group, enabled Zaibatsu to recruit and integrate professional managers. The Zaibatsu was not inhibited by a reluctance to taking on nonfamily members, a common factor in limiting the growth of a family enterprise. In fact, as a Zaibatsu empire expanded, day-to-day management was taken over more and more by professional managers. Young men were recruited by the holding company and assigned to various subsidiaries. The Zaibatsu's prestige enabled them to recruit the best graduates of the nation's leading universities. Through intensive training and work assignments, these men acquired discipline and loyalty to the family. Thus, through these means, Zaibatsu acquired decided advantages in economies of scale in capital, technology, and management.

Within this structure, the trading company took on integrative functions. It was able to tap the financial resources of the bank; it had ready access to the services of its shipping and warehousing arms. By serving as the purchasing and sales agent for all of the group's manufacturing enterprises, it was able to amass significant economies of scale in these activities. One such benefit was the fact that these trading companies, by the turn of the century, were able to establish an extensive network of branches and offices in every major market in the world. Through these offices, they engaged in commercial transactions and identified new technology and products and fed them back to the manufacturing firms they served.

By the turn of the century, Japan successfully established large-scale operations in a number of major industries, primarily by imitating Western technology. Particularly relevant from the point of view of export, was the development of a modern large-scale textile industry. For these firms, major trading companies performed extremely useful functions of procuring raw materials from abroad and exporting an important share of their growing output all over the world.

Also, throughout the decades of the 1880s and 90s, Zaibatsu trading companies had developed ingenious skills of mobilizing a large number of small industries. This was especially significant for export. Japan's struggling modern industries were hardly competitive in the world market. An important part of initial export had to come from labor-intensive cottage industries—a problem faced by many developing countries today and an extremely difficult one to overcome. The trading company provided the essential links by skillfully organizing a large number of small enterprises to produce for the export market. The relationship between the trading companies and the small firms subsequently came to be known as *Keiretsu*. (*Kei* means lineage and group and *retsu* means arranged in order, so that Keiretsu suggests an organization that is hierarchically well ordered.) The trading company supplied its Keiretsu firms with raw materials, technical and management assistance, and most important, credit. Through the trading company, the Zaibatsu's capital was allocated to small enterprises. This unique relationship between large and small enterprises gave cottage industries access to foreign markets and provided them with economies of scale to an extraordinary degree. Indeed, this organization contributed in an important way to Japan's becoming a major trading nation within three decades after emerging from the feudal system.

A unique aspect of the Keiretsu relationship was, once again, a structure that incorporated traditional social elements. The trading company's control went far beyond such tangibles as credit,

access to market, and supply of raw materials. The Keiretsu organization was hierarchical and almost always exclusive and cohesive as a group, and it was governed by a set of mutual obligations. Small enterprises vowed loyalty to the trading company,
which in return showed a paternalistic interest in them. Although exploitation of small captive suppliers by giant trading
companies was not entirely unknown, traditional values, which
stressed mercy on the part of those at the top, had an important
moderating influence.

The trading companies were ideally suited to export cheap,
labor-intensive, highly standardized products of both large-scale
as well as cottage industries, such as textiles, fabricated metals,
and inexpensive household products, for which price was the
dominant sales consideration. Within a foreign market, these
products were sold by local wholesalers and retailers. Neither
technical services nor advertising and sales promotion were
required. Of overriding importance for trading in these products
was the simple communication of information on price and volume.

The internal organization of the trading company remained
fairly simple throughout the prewar period. It was divided along
major product lines, and division managers and heads of foreign
branches were given considerable autonomy. Managers were
sent abroad for extended periods of time. The difficulty of communication limited opportunities for direct interaction between
people at foreign branches and senior management in Japan.
Thus, the chief means by which trading companies controlled
their far-flung operations was once again traditional values.
Managers felt a strong loyalty to the family-owned Honsha or the
holding company, and constant direction and supervision were
unnecessary. These men were trusted to exercise their judgment
in the best interests of the Zaibatsu. Poor commercial judgments
were inescapable, to be sure, but there were very few managers
who were indiscreet or disloyal for the sake of personal gain.

The Zaibatsu structure was not a monopoly in the nineteenth-
century American mold; rather it was an oligopoly. Each Zaibatsu was diversified and competed vigorously against other Zaibatsu. Why this was so is a tantalizing question. Certainly there
were no legal restrictions which would have discouraged the formation of a monopoly. Several different forces, however, inhibited such a development. For one thing, a strong rivalry existed
among the various cliques in the military, the bureaucracy, and

the political parties. Each had its own favorite Zaibatsu and was anxious to maintain its relative strength. Furthermore, the military and state bureaucracies were anxious to encourage a degree of competition in order to safeguard technical progress. No doubt they were also interested in checking Zaibatsu influence so that no single one would come to dominate any key industry and thereby gain inordinate political power. Another important force inhibiting monopoly was the fact that the market for most types of industrial goods grew beyond the stage where complete monopolization of any one industry would have provided real economies of scale in production and distribution, given the level of technological and managerial skills. Finally, once the Zaibatsu structure came into being, it influenced subsequent strategy, which emphasized further diversification and matching the actions of chief rivals.

The initial close ties forged between the government and Zaibatsu were perpetuated throughout the prewar era. Government influence was pervasive. The relationship between government and business in prewar Japan cannot be understood within the framework of the modern Western distinction between public and private sectors. To prewar Japanese political and business leaders, the line of demarcation did not exist in any philosophical or ideological sense. It was merely a convenience to satisfy pragmatic requirements. For all practical purposes, public and private interests were one, and they shared the risks associated with initiating and managing large-scale industrial enterprises.

The government controlled industry not by any elaborate legal means but by informal guidance supported by various forms of patronages. Indeed, influence flowed both ways. By the turn of the century Zaibatsu had become partners, patrons, and sometimes even active participants in the political process, as well as national instruments for development. Mitsui and Mitsubishi financed the two rival political parties and contracted close family ties with leading politicians and bureaucrats. The Zaibatsu's top executives floated back and forth between positions in business and in various government ministries including the Bank of Japan and the Ministry of Commerce. In fact, the central pool of high-level administrative talents in the Zaibatsu holding companies served a very useful purpose in this respect, since they shared values, traditions, and ideology with high government officials.

Strategy and Structure, 1945–1970

Defeat wiped out the hard-won economic progress Japan had made during the decades preceding the war. In 1945 Japanese industries found themselves in disarray and their environment utterly changed. Their productive capacities had been almost totally destroyed; the country was occupied and inflation was rampant. As a part of extensive economic reforms instigated by the Allied Occupation, the Zaibatsu were dissolved. Even some of their major subsidiaries, notably the Mitsui and Mitsubishi trading companies, were broken up into numerous units. The prewar structure, so painstakingly built up and so effective, was demolished.

In the immediate aftermath of the defeat, as in the early years of industrialization, the government led the way. Its initial objective was survival itself. The government selected four key industries—coal, fertilizer, power, and steel—as the industries to be revived and reconstructed first. The government allocated its scarce capital to give these industries heavy subsidies. Japanese industry got a much-needed boost by becoming a major source of supplies for the American military forces during the Korean War. And in 1952 Japan regained her independence.

From the early 1950s through the 1960s, the strategy of Japanese government and industry was well defined.[9] The objective was to build more modern industries. The strategy had three basic elements. One was to protect domestic industries against foreign competition. During much of this period, the Japanese government maintained rigid control over import and entry of foreign capital. The second element was a time-phased targeted approach toward industrial development designed to make the most efficient use of scarce capital, technology, and management. From time to time, the government chose certain industries to be developed and provided them with subsidies and special privileges. The third element in the strategy was promotion of export. Japan had always lacked most of the raw materials essential to modern industries, and the loss of her former colonies and quasi-colonies compounded the problem. Thus, to pay for import of raw materials and technologies, the government encouraged export by providing strong incentives.

In the postwar years, as in the prewar period, the government played an important role. In the postwar years, power became diffused within the bureaucracy and the business community, and certain limited aspects of the relationship between them became more formalized.[10] Nevertheless, the basic nature of the relationship remained unaltered. Direct government ownership of enterprises and even formal regulations were very limited. Rather, the Ministry of International Trade and Industry (MITI), the government's chief instrument for implementing the national strategy, generated numerous targets and plans for key industries. Although the government provided subsidies to industries in these fields, the absolute amount was rather small. What these targets and plans did was to alert financial and industrial enterprises to the sectors that the government considered important and to stamp them with the government's implicit guarantee. The government also stepped in occasionally to coordinate when major industries had key operating problems. For example, because of the lumpiness of investment characteristic in the capital-intensive industries that had already begun to dominate the Japanese economy by the late 1950s, various industries encountered a temporary overcapacity from time to time. In these situations, MITI served as the focal point for adjusting output and planning new capital investments.

Despite the pervasiveness of government influence, Japan has never had a planned economy on a classical model. Furthermore, the Japanese government has never been, in essence, a giant corporate headquarters on the model of those which direct and control multidivision companies in America. MITI did offer an extraordinary amount of consultation, advice, persuasion, and threat. But it seldom issued directives. Instead, it sought consensus, eagerly searching out the views of the private sector and incorporating them into programs. This consensus-seeking process, of course, did not eliminate frequent, vigorous, and unruly competition between the government and business for power and advantage. Sometimes, struggles and conflicts manifested themselves openly. On the one hand, bureaucrats considered themselves the guardians of Japan's national interests and often deplored the selfish motives and narrow points of view of businessmen; on the other hand, business leaders were suspicious of bureaucratic intervention wherever it failed to support their own calculations. Notwithstanding these differences, however, the leaders of government and industry shared a basic commitment throughout this period to building Japan into a leading industrial power in the world.

As in the prewar years, much of the initiative for implementing this growth strategy came from private enterprise. As a part of its catching-up process, the Japanese industries turned once again to advanced foreign technology. During the 1950s and much of the 1960s Japan was in an excellent bargaining position to obtain foreign technologies. Japan imposed almost ironclad restrictions on import and investment. Yet, given the size of a large internal market and its rapid growth rates, foreign enterprises could hardly ignore Japan. Moreover, Japan had become a major economic threat in the world economy prior to World War II, and by the end of the 1950s it was clear that the threat might soon become even greater. Moreover, most of the technology the Japanese industries were eagerly searching for during much of this period had pressed beyond the monopolistic stage. In fact, some technologies had become well diffused and a number of competing technologies were available. Confronted with this situation, foreign enterprises considered licensing. Licensing agreements would help them establish a foothold in Japan and would provide them with a valuable learning experience. The ties these agreements would establish between foreign and Japanese firms would also provide the non-Japanese enterprises with a certain amount of leverage, albeit temporary, for controlling the behavior of Japanese enterprises in the world market. Thus, between 1950 and 1972 Japanese firms entered into 17,600 licensing agreements for which they paid for $3.3 billion in royalties.[11] The technology thus obtained covered practically every field of modern industry. In the number of agreements, electric machinery led the field, followed in order by chemicals, pharmaceuticals, synthetic fibers, transportation equipment, processed foods, and iron and steel.

Judged by almost any standard, the Japanese postwar industrial strategy was successful. By the late 1960s Japan's gross national product was second only to the United States, and it was roughly equivalent to the combined G.N.P. of the rest of Asia and Latin America. By the late 1960s the output of the heavy and chemical industries accounted for 70 percent of the nation's total industrial output. In a number of industries—shipbuilding, automobiles, steel, chemicals, electronics, synthetic fiber, machinery, to name just a few—Japan was either the first or second largest producer and exporter in the non-Communist world. Table 1-1 shows the dramatic increase in Japan's share of world production. The Japanese export had become dominated by these products. (See Table 1-2 for growth of exports and changes in their composition in the postwar era.) Japan's competitive advantages in these industries lay in economy of scale in production and in a still low-cost but high-quality labor force.

To implement the postwar strategy, Japanese enterprises developed new structures and modified time-proven traditional ones. The first to be noted is the formation of the Zaikai, a unique and elusive entity. Zaikai is literally translated as business or financial community. Although the Zaikai is not an officially organized body and its membership is not clearly defined, the term generally refers to a small group of the most powerful of Japan's elite business leaders, and they often hold high offices in such powerful organizations as the Japan Federation of Economic Organization, the Japan Chamber of Commerce, and the Japan Employers' Association.

As the respected elder statesmen of the business community, they serve, individually and collectively, as the chief spokesmen for business interests. They maintain a close relationship with leaders of the ruling Liberal Democratic Party and play a critical role in mobilizing the financial resources of the business community for the party. In fact, the support of the Zaikai is considered essential to win the nomination to the premiership. These men express views formally and informally on major national issues of the day and, from time to time, mobilize the resources of the business community to support important projects in the national interest. They serve as intermediaries in resolving conflicts between business and the government or between specific industries and enterprises. They discipline industries and enterprises whose actions they do not consider in the best interests of the business community as a whole.

Two forces are believed to have been responsible for the creation of the Zaikai. First, the dissolution of the Zaibatsu destroyed a well-organized, tightly knit, and highly disciplined business elite dominated mostly by the Zaibatsu leadership, particularly of Mitsui and Mitsubishi. The business community, its power base thus diffused, found that it needed central leadership to represent its interests effectively vis-à-vis powerful external groups. Second, the business needed some kind of countervailing force to the government, particularly to the pervasive influence of the bureaucracy. In the prewar days, the Zaibatsu financed the major political parties and their leaders assumed key government posts. With the dissolution of the Zaibatsu these practices ended. The business community sought to provide an informal yet powerful check on the bureaucracy by according a special status to a small group of well-respected business leaders. This group could balance the force of the bureaucracy by maintaining close ties with the leadership of the Liberal Democratic Party to which the bureaucracy traditionally paid deference.

By the mid-1950s former Zaibatsu firms began to reestablish themselves, though in an altered form. The Allied Occupation had severed family ownership, broken up the all-powerful holding companies, and forbidden the use of the Zaibatsu names. The reforms forced each operating company to become an independent corporation, with widely dispersed stock ownership. But, by the early 1950s, the underlying conditions which had led to the original emergence of the Zaibatsu were present again in a more compelling form than ever. Japan's leading enterprises were concerned with modernizing, rebuilding, and closing the wide technical gap between themselves and the firms of other modern nations; at the same time, capital was scarce and technical and administrative expertise was limited.

The senior executives of former Zaibatsu firms saw the advantages of pooling their resources. Since family ownership was completely severed and holding companies were made illegal in the postwar era, it was impossible to regroup in the traditional manner. These men saw that new relationships had to be formed on the basis of much more limited cross-holding of stock, and on occasional interlocking directorates. Thus, they were bound by their awareness of the practical benefits to be derived from cooperation, and the deeply rooted loyalty and solidarity nurtured by the prewar family-oriented Zaibatsu system.[12]

Although the new Zaibatsu lacked tight discipline and strict central coordination, in the prewar tradition the group's bank and trading company had emerged to assume the position of leadership and a coordination function for the group. The fact that it provided capital and other essential resources to all the member companies placed it in a unique position. Both had been important in the prewar Zaibatsu. In this manner, the Mitsubishi, Mitsui, and Sumitomo groups reemerged. Though they no longer enjoyed the amount of power they had exercised in the prewar era, their new structure made various forms of cooperation possible and facilitated the pooling of scarce resources and the sharing of risks in new fields.

As Japanese business pursued its postwar strategy, another

new structure emerged in the form of bank-centered groups. The forced dissolution of the Zaibatsu, by loosening the tightly controlled economy, had encouraged the development of large manufacturing and commercial enterprises outside the Zaibatsu. These were enterprises of both prewar and postwar origins, including such well-known companies as Hitachi in electric machinery and electronics, Nissan in automobiles, Teijin in synthetic fiber, and Showa Denko in aluminum smelting and chemicals. Since new technology was available from foreign sources and managerial resources were available, these companies found that, in order to enter new fields and expand their capacities, their most serious problem was to amass the large quantities of capital they needed. Throughout the 1950s and 1960s, the stock market remained underdeveloped and could provide only a small portion of the capital needs of rapidly expanding enterprises.

Instead, their needs were met primarily by about ten large commercial banks, commonly known as the city banks. These banks served as the chief financial intermediaries to channel the high level of private savings characteristic of this period into large-scale industrial endeavors. In the process, the banks sought to establish close links with a selected number of large firms in various growth fields. Each bank gave preferential treatment to certain firms, which in return placed their deposits with the bank, thereby enhancing its relative competitive position. Out of this arrangement grew the bank-centered groups, of which the most dominant were the ones called Fuyo (Fuji Bank), Daichi-Kangin, and Sanwa. Each group consisted of a diversified cluster of manufacturing and service firms, among which there was a limited amount of cross-holding of stocks. Sometimes, in addition, a representative of a bank occupied a senior management position in a key client firm.

The bonds among these firms, however, remained a good deal looser and weaker than those that held together the reconstructed Zaibatsu groups. Unlike a Zaibatsu group, a bank-centered group lacked a clear identification and a common heritage. Often the bank and the trading company competed for leadership and hindered the development of close coordination. Nevertheless, these groups enabled non-Zaibatsu firms to pool their resources and to share risks to an extent that would otherwise have been difficult.

The reconstituted Zaibatsu groups and the bank-centered

groups competed vigorously, each attempting to participate in every major growth field. The Zaibatsu had had a history of oligopolistic rivalry. In addition, postwar economic reforms and rapid economic growth opened up fresh opportunities for non-Zaibatsu firms. Throughout the 1950s and well into the 1960s, the types of technology sought by Japanese enterprises were relatively mature ones and were available from a number of different sources. To a group which already had diversified interests, there was considerable risk in failing to match a rival's entry into a major new field, because the rival group's move would pose a threat to the existing equilibrium. Then, too, the competitive position of a bank depended, to an important degree, on the strength of its affiliated companies. Once committed to a given field, an enterprise competed vigorously for a greater share of the market in order to increase its capacity and reap the benefits of the economy of scale. In critical industries, market share was crucial, since it was the standard criterion in MITI's formula for approving capacity expansion.

There were also noneconomic incentives for competition among these groups. The importance the Japanese historically attach to the collectivity encouraged such competition. Though rivalry among firms within a particular group became quite intense at times, each group developed a high degree of solidarity when confronted with external threats. Since size and rate of growth were the major criteria for determining the relative positions of the groups, each group was strongly motivated to meet moves into new fields by rival groups.

Two types of structural adaptation took place in relation to the implementation of export strategy. First was the resurgence of trading companies on a much larger scale and with more diversified product lines. As Japanese industries increased their competitive ability, the volume of Japanese export soared, and the range of products widened. Six trading companies became dominant. Though Mitsubishi and Mitsui trading companies were not as powerful as they had been before the war, they still vied for first place. Marubeni and C. Itoh, which had once specialized in textiles, and Nissho-Iwai, which had once specialized in metals, moved into the vacuum created by the dissolution of Zaibatsu in the immediate aftermath of the war and successfully diversified into other lines, thereby becoming *Sogo Shosha* or general trading companies. The Sumitomo Trading Company, though of much more recent origin than either Mitsui or Mitsubishi, grew rapidly with the strong support of the Sumitomo group.

In 1973 the combined sales of these six companies reached ¥21,520 billion or $76.8 billion—about 20 percent of Japan's G.N.P. (See Table 1-3 for details.) Reflecting the change in the structure of Japanese industry, their product mix had undergone some change. There was a decline in the relative importance of textiles and sundry goods and a gain in that of steel, nonferrous metals, chemicals, standard machinery, and construction materials. (See Table 1-4 for major product categories of the two leading trading companies in 1973.)

As the composition of Japanese export changed in favor of the products of capital-intensive and technological industries, trading companies saw the need and the opportunity to restructure the Keiretsu. What they did was link the large-scale oligopolistic enterprises which produced intermediate materials to the small enterprises which performed various downstream operations. In synthetic fiber, for example, they integrated large fiber manufacturers with firms performing spinning, weaving, dyeing, and apparel manufacturing. In steel, Keiretsu involved large steel manufacturers and various fabricators, for whom the trading company served as a critical intermediary. To secure these ties, trading companies used the familiar techniques of partial equity ownership, management and technical assistance, and credit extension. At the end of March 1974 the big six held stock in a total of 5,390 companies, of which 1,848 were listed on stock exchanges. They were the largest stockholders in 1,057 companies, which had a combined capitalization of $440 billion and total sales of $6,250 billion—about 30 percent of the combined sales of the parent companies. Credit extension was an even more important means of Keiretsu control. The six extended a total trade credit to suppliers and customers of $7,400 billion, a sum that exceeded the total loans made by the largest Japanese commercial bank by a margin of $2,700 billion. To be sure, not all this money went to Keiretsu companies, but a good part of it did.

Keiretsu gave the leading trading companies flexibility in its mix of products for the export market. Depending on the needs of a particular customer, a trading company was able to export fiber directly from large manufacturers, yarn from its associated spinning firms, or woven cloth or even clothing made by its

Keiretsu textile manufacturers. Certainly, the traditional social bond governing the Keiretsu survived the war and all the changes subsequent to it.

To achieve further market penetration in the postwar decades, the leading trading companies expanded and strengthened their international networks. At the end of March 31, 1973, for example, Mitsubishi, the largest of the six, had the following networks outside Japan to carry out its trading activities: 14 branches, 23 subsidiaries, and 82 other offices. To staff these offices, it maintained 763 expatriate managers from Japan and 2,460 foreign nationals. (See Table 1-5 for similar data on other trading companies.) In addition to their main functions of buying, selling, and credit extension, these foreign offices served various other purposes, including that of gathering information on new products and technology, not only for headquarters but also for the company's manufacturing clients.

The need for another type of structural adjustment came about when Japanese industries began to emphasize export of goods that required extensive marketing efforts or technical services or both. Trading companies were ill equipped to provide either marketing or technical services. Their forte lay in managing large-scale transactions involving highly standard goods for which price was the primary consideration. Typically, they relied on local wholesalers for distribution within a foreign market and seldom involved themselves beyond the level of primary wholesalers.

Successful export of the new kinds of consumer goods, such as consumer electronics, cameras, motorcycles, and automobiles, however, required intensive marketing efforts, particularly if the products were to be marketed under the company's own brand name. Advertising and sales promotions were vital; dealer organizations had to be built and servicing provided. The information requirements for such functions were much more complex than those for the sale of standard commodities. Consumer taste had to be investigated, fashion trends ascertained, and sales of different models and types of products closely monitored. For technical products, individual customer requirements had to be gauged, special designs incorporated, and technical services provided. To satisfy technical and marketing requirements, exporters of such products had to build enduring relationships in the marketplace and to assure the smooth flow of information between those engaged in marketing activities in the foreign countries and various elements at corporate headquarters.

In order to satisfy these requirements, leading manufacturers established sales subsidiaries abroad to perform marketing and technical tasks. Between 1952 and 1973, 50 leading firms dealing in automobiles and motorcycles, electrical machinery, precision instruments, and nonelectrical machinery established 317 sales subsidiaries in major export markets. (See Table 1-6 for details.) In view of the requirements for close control over marketing and technical activities as well as for frequent communication between the local unit and headquarters, it is not surprising to find that nearly 71 percent of these subsidiaries were wholly owned, and another 16 percent majority owned.

Erosion of the Traditional Strategy

The very success Japan achieved led to a new environment which, by the end of the 1960s, began to demand a fundamental reassessment of her postwar strategy. Challenging the very premises of the Japanese strategy, some of these forces began to manifest themselves by the early 1960s, others only in the late 1960s. But by the early 1970s, they all began to converge, threatening the effectiveness of Japanese export strategy; the policy of protecting home markets against foreign competition; and the Japanese ability to procure essential raw materials abroad.

Exports. The threat to Japanese exports came partly from the actions of foreign governments. The governments of both developing and developed countries were imposing more and more restrictions on Japanese imports. Most developing countries, anxious to encourage their own industries, have pursued policies of import substitution for some time. Their efforts, some of which had originated several decades earlier, intensified in the 1950s and early 1960s, just as Japanese manufacturing enterprises began to establish a strong export position. Although different countries adopted different specific measures, their basic approach was well tested and familiar. Typically, a government systematically scanned the products that could be manufactured locally and imposed high tariffs and other restrictions to discourage or even prohibit their import. At the same time, it offered attractive incentives to anyone interested in establishing local maufacturing or assembly plants.

Japanese export was particularly vulnerable to these pressures, since so much of it consisted of standard consumer products, with a particular emphasis on lower price lines. The first target of import substitution was usually the last stage of the production of consumer goods, including the manufacture of textiles or simple metal products, the packaging of drugs and toiletries, and the assembly of consumer durables such as radios, television sets, and refrigerators.

In the mid-1960s, Japanese exports began to encounter a different sort of threat in advanced countries, notably the United States. The rapid shift of Japanese export to the types of product in which, traditionally, U.S. industries were strong—steel, automobiles, consumer electronics products, and chemicals, for example—elicited cries for restriction from U.S. manufacturers of these products. Tensions heightened in the early 1970s as the Japanese trade surplus with the United States reached the highest levels ever. In 1971 it was $3.2 billion, almost triple the previous peak. In 1972 it reached $4.2 billion. In contrast to the explicit measures typical of the import substitution policies of developing countries, restrictions against import into the United States took subtle forms, such as investigations for possible violations of U.S. antidumping regulations and political pressures to accept voluntary restraints and quotas. From time to time, these measures directly affected or at least seriously threatened a wide spectrum of products, including television sets, steel, ball bearings, and automobiles—all of them types of product for which continued access to markets was important. And the situation in Europe was no more encouraging than that in the United States.

Another grave source of trouble for Japan's export strategy was a decline in the competitive ability of Japanese industries. Here too, several different forces were converging. Wage levels in Japan were rising rapidly. In the early 1960s, Japan started to experience a labor shortage for the first time. Rapid growth had exhausted what had been a large reservoir of unemployed and underemployed workers. From 1961 on, the unemployment rate never exceeded 1.5 percent of the labor force. There was a particularly acute shortage of young workers in their middle-to-late teens. One of Japan's distinct advantages in the world market had traditionally been her abundance of young workers with manual skills and discipline. The seniority-based wage system in Japan made these workers especially attractive to employers. Two booming decades, however, steadily reduced the number of junior high school graduates available for work. During the

1950s, over a third of the graduating class entered the labor market every year. During the first half of the 1960s, the percentage of those entering the labor market declined to less than a quarter; and during the next few years it declined still further to 15 percent. Company recruiters became extremely competitive, combing the country in search of "golden eggs," as the young workers came to be known.

Because of the labor shortage, the average wage more than doubled during the 1960s. The tempo of increases accelerated in the early 1970s. Between 1970 and 1973, the average rate of increase exceeded 18 percent a year, and in 1974, in the so-called spring offensive, when unions present their annual demands to management, the average increase in wages over those of the preceding year reached an unprecedented 30 percent. Though any international comparison of wage rates is hazardous at best, it is fairly safe to assume that by 1974 the wage level in Japan had reached or exceeded that of Europe.

The impact of the labor shortage was not confined to wage levels. In addition, the wage gap between various age levels narrowed. Furthermore, the wage difference that once existed between large and small enterprises melted away—a fact with special implications for large firms which had capitalized on that difference by having smaller affiliated firms with low wages perform labor-intensive activities. Temporary workers, who once provided an important escape hatch for large Japanese enterprises saddled with the rigidities of permanent employment, had all but disappeared. Finally, the labor shortage had weakened the discipline of the work force, particularly of younger workers. The number of work hours gradually declined and annual vacations and the five-day work week were becoming widely accepted. By 1973 over half of all enterprises with 1,000 employees or more had adopted, at least partially, the five-day week.[13]

A second force beginning to weaken the international competitiveness of Japanese industries was a steep rise in the costs associated with capacity expansion within Japan in heavy and chemical industries. This stemmed, in part, from the scarcity of land suitable for industrial use. By the 1960s attractive sites had long since been snapped up, and whatever was still available had become extremely expensive. Adding further to costs was a growing public concern about the deterioration of the environment. By the early 1970s postwar economic growth and the shift toward heavy and chemical industries had resulted in widespread destruction of the environment and a worsening of the quality of life. Japan is a small country, about 5 percent the size of the United States, with a population roughly half that of the United States. Because of the scarcity of flat land, the three industrial areas—those around greater Tokyo, Osaka, and Ise Bay—make up less than a third of Japan's land area; yet in 1974 they had more than half her population, produced nearly three quarters of her manufactures, and consumed 64 percent of her energy. Environmental problems were similarly concentrated. For example, in 1973 a narrow strip of industrial land between Tokyo and Yokohama was exposed to over 6,000,000 tons of sulphuric acid annually, or 127 tons per square mile—more than ten times the national average.

Until the early 1970s few positive actions were taken to protect the environment. The central government showed little concern. Air and water pollution, traffic congestion, and noise levels were appalling in major industrial centers. In the late 1960s citizens' movements sprang up to press for protection of the environment. For such a sustained grass roots movement to arise without any authoritarian regimentation was a new social phenomenon in Japan. Nevertheless, by 1970 there were nearly 300 citizens' organizations actively committed to environmental protection.[14] Between 1966 and 1970 the annual number of formal complaints made to local governments about environmental problems increased from 20,502 to 63,433.

This concern about the environment caused public sentiment to shift gradually away from the single-minded commitment to economic growth that had characterized the decades of the 1950s and 1960s. Public sentiment, in fact, began to turn against business itself, particularly giant enterprises. A tangible manifestation of the public's hostility was its active, even violent opposition to the building of new plants with potential for damaging the environment. This local attitude made it all but impossible to build major plants in such industries as chemicals, steel, petroleum, and petrochemicals. By the early 1970s Japan's major industrial firms could hardly find room for expansion within the country. Even if a firm managed to find an appropriate plant site, it had to be prepared to spend a large sum of money to meet the extremely rigorous pollution control requirements imposed by the local community.

Two rounds of yen revaluation further damaged Japanese

competitive ability in the export market. In 1971 the yen, which had been fixed for more than two decades at the exchange rate of ¥360 to $1.00, was revalued and again in 1973. The exchange rate thereafter fluctuated between ¥280 and ¥300 to $1.00. The two rounds of revaluation, combined with the rising wage levels, seriously undermined the competitive ability of export-oriented Japanese manufacturing industries.[15]

Among these industries the high-energy-consuming ones were also hard hit by the dramatic increases in petroleum prices in 1973. The international competitiveness of steel, aluminum refining, automobiles, and chemicals suffered a decline. Of all the advanced nations, Japan depends most heavily on oil as a source of energy. And in 1974 alone her nine power companies increased their rates for industrial use by as much as 75 percent.

Protection of the domestic market. In the early 1950s, when the task of rebuilding industry had begun in earnest, the Japanese government had imposed rigid restriction. Foreigners were discouraged by these legal restrictions and also by Japan's distinctive business system, complex marketing practices, and unfamiliar culture. Through the early 1960s, imports and the entry of capital stayed extremely low.[16] But Japan's rapidly expanding internal market and intense penetration of the world market caused other nations, particularly the United States, to press Japan to liberalize restrictions. And when Japan joined the O.E.C.D. in 1964, she had to agree to the gradual removal of the restrictions. By the late 1960s, import and capital liberalization had actually come to be in the best interests of Japan's major industries. There were two primary reasons for this.

First, by this time Japanese export, particularly to the United States, had become dominated by the products of capital-intensive, oligopolistic industries in which economy of scale was a central consideration. Certain peculiarities of the Japanese situation—notably a heavy reliance on debt with high fixed charges, and permanent employment—added further pressure for capacity utilization. Export had become, by then, a built-in element in capacity planning, so that any disruption of exports was extremely costly. Furthermore, successful marketing of these products required close and sustained contacts with customers, involving dealer and service organizations, advertising, and promotion. At least some of the costs associated with these activities were also fixed. Moreover, having successfully built modern industries, the Japanese could hardly return to the production of traditional labor-intensive products without making sacrifices in their standard of living which were unacceptable in any situation short of a national emergency.

The second reason was changing technological needs of the Japanese industries which had become apparent by the late 1960s. Japanese industries, having mastered most of the mature technologies, began to seek new technological frontiers. Innovative technologies were important if the industries were to diversify into new growth fields. Unlike the standard technologies in chemicals, metal processing, home appliances, and automobiles, such technologies were often monopolistic. The foreign firms which had developed them demanded much more than mere licensing agreements from the Japanese. They were interested in obtaining a permanent foothold in the Japanese market. This situation substantially weakened Japan's once-strong bargaining position.

For these reasons, then, in the national debates to determine the timing and degree of import and capital liberalization, the Zaikai leadership took a liberal stance, pressing the conservative MITI for extensive liberalization. The MITI, however, fearful that liberalization might erode its power, was reluctant and mobilized the support of industries it judged to be particularly vulnerable to foreign competition. Eventually, nevertheless, a carefully controlled program of liberalization was formulated and implemented. By 1970 almost all import restrictions had been removed; by 1973, with very few exceptions, capital liberalization was complete as well.

By the early 1970s, Japanese manufacturers, like their U.S. and European counterparts, had begun to face increased foreign competition in their home markets. For the first time, they had to be prepared to protect their own flanks as they exploited market opportunities abroad. No longer was the home market a secure sanctuary reserved for Japanese enterprises. The threat of retaliation in their home market by major foreign competitors began to limit freedom of action Japanese enterprises had once enjoyed abroad.

Procurement of raw materials. Finally, by the end of the 1960s the materials strategy Japan had followed throughout the 1950s and 1960s—that of procuring needed raw materials from foreign sources—was in danger. Japan had little choice. In most of the raw-material industries, particularly in minerals, the barriers to entry were too high during much of this period for Japanese industries to overcome. For most mineral resources, however, world market conditions were such that Japan was able to obtain favorable terms by using her rapidly growing demand as leverage. By 1970, however, these conditions had begun to change.

Furthermore, by 1970 Japan had become one of the world's largest consumers of key raw materials (see Table 1-7). Japan consumed, for example, 9 percent of the petroleum used in the non-Communist world, 14 percent of the copper, 11 percent of the aluminum, and 16 percent of the iron ores. Moreover, she had to import 76 percent of her copper, 79 percent of her coking coal, 98 percent of her petroleum, and 100 percent of her aluminum (see Table 1-8). Procuring these raw materials through the traditional method of bulk buying had become increasingly difficult. More important, Japan's heightened dependence on foreign sources for these critical materials increased the risk of continuing to depend on the traditional method. The oil crisis in 1973 was a sobering reminder to Japan of her vulnerability. It dealt a severe blow to the assumption implicit in her past strategy that resources would always be readily available at low cost.

As a result of all these developments, by the early 1970s the setting in which Japanese industries operated had changed drastically, forcing them to alter their strategy in two important ways. First, Japan's enterprises became increasingly interested in promoting their own resource exploration and development. The result was a significant increase in the number of overseas ventures, Japanese-owned and managed, dealing in aluminum, copper, iron ores, petroleum, pulp, agricultural products, fish, and other materials. Second, Japanese industries plunged into the establishment of manufacturing facilities abroad, some designed primarily to defend the export market, others to gain access to low-cost labor. Through such facilities, Japanese firms also stepped up their efforts to gain favored access to advanced technology, low-cost energy, and suitable plant sites.

Though still in the early stage, the new strategy was being vigorously implemented. Although the absolute sum of Japanese foreign direct investment in 1973 was only about 5 percent as much as that of the United States, the growth rate was soaring. (See Table 1-9.) During 1971 and 1972 the total book value of overseas investment nearly doubled. Nearly 39 percent of it went into the development of minerals, agriculture, and fisheries, 26 percent into manufacturing, and 12 percent into commerce. The remaining 23 percent was divided among construction, finance, and other service-related activities. (Details are presented in Table 1-9.)

Japanese investment was divided almost equally between advanced and developing countries, with the advanced countries accounting for roughly 54 percent. Europe was the site for $1,660 million,[17] the United States $1,550 million, Asia $1,390 million, Latin America $990 million, the Middle East $610 million, Oceania $430 million, and Africa $158 million.

Table 1-1. Value of output of selected products as a percentage of the non-Communist world output, 1965 and 1971

PRODUCT	1965	1971
Steel	13	22
Petrochemicals	12	18
Paper and pulp	8	11
Synthetic fiber	20	21
Automobiles	8	18
Electronics	6	14
Consumer electronics	13	38
Shipbuilding	46	50
Machinery	9	18

Source: Adapted from *Kogin chosa* Report No. 1, 1974, p. 6.

Table 1-2. Japan's exports by principal commodity, selected years, 1953–73

PRODUCT	THOUSANDS OF DOLLARS	PERCENTAGE OF TOTAL	THOUSANDS OF DOLLARS	PERCENTAGE OF TOTAL	THOUSANDS OF DOLLARS	PERCENTAGE OF TOTAL
	1953		*1957*		*1960*	
Textiles	460,336	36.1	1,015,083	35.5	1,223,352	30.1
Chemicals	72,217	5.7	135,619	4.7	181,089	4.4
Nonferrous machinery	62,348	4.9	129,204	4.5	168,988	4.1
Iron and steel	192,075	15.1	326,005	11.4	568,393	14.0
Machinery	189,430	14.9	633,567	22.1	1,035,086	25.5
Foodstuffs	120,232	9.4	173,360	6.1	255,932	6.3
Other	178,210	14.0	445,180	15.5	621,697	15.3
Total	1,274,843	100.0	2,858,018	100.0	4,054,537	100.0
	1965		*1970*		*1973*	
Textiles	1,581,746	18.7	2,407,524	12.5	3,278,802	8.9
Chemicals	546,911	6.5	1,234,462	6.4	2,147,026	5.8
Nonferrous machinery	265,108	3.1	372,376	1.9	571,264	1.5
Iron and steel	1,718,164	20.3	3,805,336	19.7	6,821,372	18.5
Machinery	2,975,488	35.2	8,941,266	46.3	20,364,776	55.1
Foodstuffs	343,843	4.0	647,744	3.3	841,380	2.3
Other	1,020,482	12.1	1,908,978	9.8	2,905,351	7.8
Total	8,451,742	100.0	19,317,689	100.0	36,929,971	100.0

Source: Economics Statistics Annual, 1973 (Tokyo: The Bank of Japan), pp. 199–200.

Table 1-3. The six largest trading companies, 1973

NAME	TOTAL SALES (¥ BILLION)	NET PROFIT (¥ BILLION)	TOTAL NUMBER OF EMPLOYEES
Mitsubishi	612	31.2	10,001
Mitsui	574	28.9	10,948
Marubeni	361	30.4	8,039
C. Itoh	340	32.7	7,454
Sumitomo	312	17.3	5,564
Nissho-Iwai	297	6.8	7,096

Source: Compiled from annual reports of the companies.

Table 1-4. Product categories of the two leading trading companies (in percent)

MITSUBISHI [a] CATEGORY		MITSUI CATEGORY	
Machinery	20.4	Machinery	18.6
Iron and steel	19.4	Metals	33.6
Foodstuffs	12.7	Foodstuffs	13.6
Nonferrous Metals	11.1		
Textiles	9.8	Textiles	9.5
Fuel	7.9		
Chemicals	7.2	Chemicals	10.8
Construction Materials	6.8		
Other	4.2	Other	13.9

Source: Company records.
[a] Because of rounding, Mitsubishi percentages do not add exactly to 100 percent.

Table 1-5. The multinational commercial presence of the 10 leading trading companies, March 31, 1973 [a]

COMPANY	BRANCHES	WHOLLY-OWNED SUBSIDIARIES	SUBUNITS OF THE BRANCHES OR BRANCHES OF THE SUBSIDIARIES	NUMBER OF PERSONNEL FROM THE PARENT COMPANY	NUMBER OF LOCAL PERSONNEL
Mitsubishi	14	23	82	763	2,460
Mitsui	15	20	79	802	2,133
Marubeni	15	17	65	592	2,041
C. Itoh	8	11	90	584	1,500
Nissho-Iwai	5	12	87	560	1,120
Sumitomo	8	10	68	476	973
Tomen	9	11	55	334	632
Nichimen	9	12	46	306	572
Kanematsu-Gosho	6	9	44	330	850
Ataka	6	7	50	234	407

Source: Company records.

[a] These entities include only those established for general trading.

Table 1-6. Number of foreign sales subsidiaries established by 50 leading manufacturing firms in selected industries, by geographic area, 1951–73

INDUSTRY	NORTH AMERICA	WESTERN EUROPE	ASIA	LATIN AMERICA	MIDDLE EAST	OCEANIA	AFRICA	TOTAL
Electric machineries	29	32	22	11	1	4	5	99
Automobiles and motorcycles	15	8	16	12	2	3	5	56
Nonelectric machineries	27	18	19	11	3	1	0	79
Precision instruments	19	12	9	6	0	0	0	46
Total	90	70	66	40	6	8	10	290

Table 1-7. Consumption of key raw materials in Japan, 1960 and 1970

RESOURCE	UNIT	1960	1970	PERCENT AVERAGE ANNUAL RATE OF INCREASE
Copper	1,000 tons	320	833	10.0
Lead	1,000 tons	108	213	7.0
Aluminum	1,000 tons	297	880	19.0
Iron ore	1,000 tons	21,100	111,000	18.1
Coking coal	1,000 tons	17,500	59,300	13.0
Petroleum	Kiloliter	29,500	185,500	20.4
Natural gas	1,000 cubic meters	773,000	3,662,000	16.9

Source: Adapted from *Shigen mondai no tenbo* (White paper on natural resources; Tokyo: Ministry of International Trade and Industry, 1971), pp. 7–9.

Table 1-8. Imports as a percentage of the total consumption of selected raw materials, 1960 and 1970

RESOURCE	1960	1970
Copper	50.6	75.6
Lead	54.6	54.6
Aluminum	100.0	100.0
Iron ore	68.0	87.9
Coking coal	35.8	78.5
Petroleum	98.6	97.7
Natural gas	0	34.8

Source: Adapted from *Shigen mondai no tenbo* (White paper on natural resources; Tokyo: Ministry of International Trade and Industry, 1971), p. 10.

Table 1-9. Annual foreign direct investment, 1951–72

YEAR	THOUSANDS OF DOLLARS	PERCENTAGE OF TOTAL INVESTMENT
Prior to 1961	$ 283,045	4.2
1961	164,227	2.4
1962	98,252	1.5
1963	125,729	1.9
1964	118,540	1.8
1965	159,378	2.3
1966	227,091	3.3
1967	274,521	4.0
1968	556,689	8.2
1969	665,046	9.8
1970	904,177	13.4
1971	858,274	12.7
1972	2,337,874	34.5
Total	$6,772,845	100.0

Source: *Keizai Kyoryoku no genjo to mondaiten* (The current status and prospect of economic cooperation; Tokyo: Ministry of International Trade and Industry, 1973), p. 629.

2. Ventures in Raw Materials

Although Japan had been for some time a major consumer and processor of key minerals such as oil, aluminum, and copper, it was not until in the late 1960s that her industries began to turn their attention in earnest to developing raw material sources abroad at their own initiative and risk. The catching-up process, which was all but completed by that time in the manufacturing industries, was just beginning in raw materials. Unlike the steel, chemical, automobile, and electronics industries, which had grown up as national industries, a handful of giant enterprises has controlled the raw material industries for some time. Eight companies in copper, seven in oil, and six in aluminum have maintained a tight grip on their respective industries. These enterprises are not only multinational in the scope of their activities, but their control extended to every stage of operations from the exploration for the minerals to the marketing of finished products. The international firms have created formidable barriers of entry.

Indeed, the gap between these international giants and the still struggling Japanese raw materials industries remains wide. In oil, for example, the foreign direct investment of U.S. companies exceeded $23 billion at the end of 1973 as compared to less than $1.6 billion for Japanese firms. A few of the American and European multinational enterprises in raw materials began to evolve almost a century before their Japanese counterparts. The Standard Oil Trust, for example, had already begun its export activities when Japan was barely emerging from feudal times.

Taking into account, then, that in the mid-1970s Japanese raw material ventures abroad were both small and young, I shall search, in this chapter, for historical parallels between the pattern of Japanese development and that of U.S. and European

33

multinational enterprises in raw materials. Since Japanese industrial development as a whole had been characterized by certain
unique attributes, a relevant question to be raised in this regard
is whether or not Japanese raw materials ventures have been
pursuing a distinctive course of development.

For detailed analysis, I have singled out oil. Oil exploration
and development is the most important element in the Japanese
raw materials investment abroad. Moreover, despite its recent
origin, the Japanese experience in oil has been more extensive
than in other minerals. Furthermore, the industry lends itself
well to an examination of the role of government. Because of
the strategic value of oil, the government has played a much
more direct and important role than in similar ventures in other
raw material fields.

In some ways, despite its brevity, the history of Japan's oil
ventures is closely parallel to that of oil ventures originating in
other countries. In venturing abroad, the Japanese oil industry,
like many of its predecessors from other countries began as a
total outsider. Not surprisingly, it started out with some unique
features, but soon its strategy began to take on some of the familiar elements that had been widely observed among the international companies, and by the mid-1970s there were clear signs
that the strategy of the Japanese oil industry had started irrevo-
cably on the course toward convergence.

Nevertheless, certain distinctive elements resulting from the
unique Japanese economic, industrial, and social systems, continue to set the Japanese development clearly apart from that of
U.S. or European oil enterprises. These distinctions, however,
have manifested themselves not in strategy, but in the structure
that has emerged to implement strategy. In this pattern of structural responses, a number of institutional elements that are
uniquely Japanese have played a central role.

Evolution of the Japanese Oil Industry

A common use of oil in Japan began after 1868. Among the
many innovative products of Western civilization introduced
right after the Meiji Restoration was the kerosene lamp, and it
soon became popular. The major oil supplier was Standard Oil.
Its virtual monopoly, however, was soon challenged by Russian
oil produced by Rothchilds.

The increasing commercial value of oil caused a large number
of individual prospectors to explore domestic reserves along the

coast of the Japan Sea. The usual process of shakedown and consolidation followed, and by the 1880s two Japanese oil firms had emerged. Despite their very small scale, these firms were vertically integrated from production of crude oil through refining to marketing. From the beginning, handicapped by their limited scale, crude technology, and inexperience in marketing, the two Japanese companies had a hard time competing against imported products. Shortly after the turn of the century, Japan, along with other Asian markets, was subjected to price skirmishes between the two companies—Standard Oil and Royal Dutch/Shell—which dominated the entire region.

World War I brought some fundamental changes in the world oil industry. The importance of oil for military and industrial use was by then well recognized. Consumption increased rapidly, and the big oil companies searched aggressively for new oil fields. There were a number of major discoveries, and between 1914 and 1921 annual production of crude oil increased from 400 million to 700,000 million barrels. The foreign companies, with their great economy of scale, flooded the Japanese market.

By the end of World War I, domestic oil resources in Japan were rapidly depleting, compelling the two Japanese oil companies to make a fundamental shift in strategy: to discontinue production of crude oil in Japan and to concentrate only on the refining and marketing, relying on imported crude oil. The barriers to entry into crude production outside Japan were too enormous for these small struggling Japanese firms to overcome. Initially, Japanese refineries bought their crude supplies from a variety of foreign sources, but by the 1930s Standard Oil of California, Standard Vacuum, and Royal Dutch/Shell emerged as the dominant suppliers. Others included Associated Oil, Union Oil, and Richfield.

Until the early 1930s the oil industry was considered unimportant. The government showed little interest in its development. Coal remained the most important source of energy. As late as 1935 coal provided 62 percent of the Japanese total energy needs, while oil provided only 9 percent. The total oil import for that year of 26 million barrels would have been used up in less than five days in 1973. Because of its marginal strategic value and the government's lack of interest, the Zaibatsu did not enter oil except for one small effort by Mitsubishi in the 1930s. Major Zaibatsu, particularly Mitsui and Sumitomo had major and highly profitable coal mining interests which further dampened their enthusiasm for oil. The first tangible manifestation of the government's interest in the strategic importance of oil was the passage of the Petroleum Industry Law in 1934. By the late 1930s government control over the industry increased substantially. Two dozen or so small refineries were consolidated into eight large ones, and their entire output was diverted to war efforts.

After the war, the Allied occupation authority did not allow Japanese oil refineries to operate again until 1949. Facilities had been totally destroyed, technology was hopelessly backward, and the industry was desperately short of capital. Not included as one of the strategic industries essential for immediate postwar reconstruction, the oil industry had to struggle without special government assistance. The only feasible way for Japanese oil interests to overcome entry barriers was to form partnerships with foreign companies. At the active encouragement of the U.S. occupation authority, a way was cleared for several Japanese companies to form joint ventures with foreign oil companies, including Caltex, Exxon, Mobil, Getty, Union Oil, and Shell.[1]

In the 1950s, in response to the rapidly growing demand for petroleum products in Japan, a dozen or so new refineries came into being, almost all of them wholly owned by Japanese interests. To distinguish them from foreign affiliates, these Japanese-owned refineries came to be known as national companies. Among these new entrants, Zaibatsu groups were once again conspicuously missing. This was partly because coal remained the dominant source of energy throughout the 1950s. Furthermore, since the petroleum refining field was already crowded with established firms, Zaibatsu firms moved into other areas which offered better and fresher opportunities. Finally, the loss of central direction deterred the postwar Zaibatsu groups from making large-scale entry into fields where they had no previous experience. Former Zaibatsu subsidiaries which were independent felt that there was greater opportunity and less risk involved in expanding into lines related to their own. Thus, textile companies that had formerly specialized in rayon entered into nylon and polyester fibers; chemical firms moved into petrochemicals; manufacturers of standard electrical industrial machineries expanded into home appliances.

From the mid-1950s on, a rapidly growing demand for petroleum presented frequent opportunities for refineries in Japan to expand their capacities. Because the economies of scale played so important a role in oil refining, there were decided advantages in being able to sustain a high rate of capacity expansion. Without Zaibatsu ties or strong banking connections, however, many of the so-called national companies were at a serious disadvantage compared with foreign affiliates whose parent companies provided them with the needed funds. Almost in desperation, the national firms turned to foreign oil companies for loans. The foreign oil companies, particularly those without a foothold in Japan, were anxious to use credit extension as a means to obtain long-term supply contracts with the national companies and thereby gain access to the rapidly growing Japanese market, a market that was by this time hedged with restrictions against foreign companies. Thus between 1958 and 1963 the national companies borrowed a total of $171 million from foreign oil companies and in return the national companies signed three- to five-year supply contracts with various international oil companies.[2]

During the 1950s, MITI tightly controlled the import of crude oil through foreign exchange allocations. Although MITI did encourage the development of national refineries, its efforts were moderated by its commitment to protect the domestic coal industry, which, though declining in importance, was still the predominant source of energy in Japan. Thus, during this period MITI tried to maintain a precarious balance.

In the early 1960s, however, MITI began to make active commitment to the development of the Japanese-owned refineries. For one thing, by 1960, it had become apparent that oil would replace coal as the primary source of energy. Between 1955 and 1960 the relative use of oil as a source of energy had increased from 22 percent to nearly 38 percent, while that of coal had declined from 52 percent to 41 percent.[3] This was of special concern to MITI, since Japan had to rely for all oil supplies on foreign sources. Moreover, by 1960 over 70 percent of imported oil was tied to specific foreign companies either through ownership or through loan arrangements. Also by 1960 it was becoming increasingly apparent to MITI officials that international pressures would soon force Japan to remove import restrictions on oil. They recognized, however, that because of the strategic importance of oil they would continue to need some instrument of control. This recognition led in 1962 to the enactment of the Petroleum Industry Law, which, among other things, empowered MITI to approve new entries into refining and capacity expansion. MITI's strategy for the oil industry emerged quite explicitly in the early 1960s—to contain foreign influence and to encourage the growth of national refineries. During the decade that followed, MITI made frequent, though not always effective, use of the law to accomplish these purposes.

Japanese Oil Ventures Abroad

During the 1950s the Japanese oil industry was not in a position to consider seriously the possibility of expanding into exploration, development, and production of crude oil. Since Japan had no domestic reserves, this would have meant venturing abroad. The Japanese affiliates of foreign oil companies were constrained from seeking upward integration on their own. The national companies were barely able to overcome the entry barriers at the refining stage and were experiencing difficulties in amassing the financial resources to keep up with expansion of refining capacities to meet the rapidly growing demand.

The first Japanese oil exploration project abroad was undertaken in the mid-1950s by a successful entrepreneur by the name of Taro Yamashita. Yamashita, a total stranger to the oil industry, came from a successful and colorful career as a businessman. He was not in the typical mold of the professional managers who had come to dominate Japan's large business establishments in the postwar era. Neither was he a part of the powerful Zaikai, although his friendship with several prominent business leaders put him on the fringe of it.

During his nearly fifty years in business, which included several colossal failures, he started a number of very successful ventures both in Japan and in Manchuria during the 1930s and early 1940s. Like so many who had pioneered in the oil business in other countries, he was daring and speculative. He was, furthermore, free from the organizational constraints that limited his contemporaries in large professionally managed enterprises.

By the mid-1950s, the importance of oil was becoming increasingly apparent. His motive was not pecuniary alone. Yamashita, who shared with many of his contemporaries a peculiar blend of patriotism and nationalism, was concerned about Japan's total dependence for crude oil on a handful of foreign companies. By initiating oil exploration he was able to bring together his quest for private gain and his desire to alleviate a critical national need.[4] His ideology was reminiscent of that of the early Meiji entrepreneurs.

In 1955 Yamashita went to Saudi Arabia with a letter of in-

troduction to the king from the Japanese Prime Minister Ishiba-
shi. He negotiated an agreement with Saudi Arabia in 1957—and
with Kuwait shortly afterwards—to explore in the neutral zone
off the coast of Saudi Arabia and Kuwait. In 1958 he formed the
Arabian Oil Company with 10 percent equity participation each
by the governments of Saudi Arabia and Kuwait.

If such a peculiar blend of patriotism and nationalism is an uncommon motive for oil exploration, what followed was even
more peculiarly Japanese. To raise money at home, Yamashita
sought the endorsement and support of a few of the Zaikai
leaders with whom he had been friends for many years. In this
endeavor he appealed to their patriotism by stirring their concern over Japan's total dependence on foreign controlled
sources for oil. His task was not easy. It must be kept in mind
that this took place in 1958, a short six years after Japan had
regained her independence, and rapid economic growth had
just begun to gain momentum. Japanese industries were fran-
tically entering new fields and expanding their capacities in already existing fields. To most businessmen preoccupied with internal growth, Saudi Arabia and Kuwait seemed remote and oil
exploration too speculative. Yamashita later recalled that most of
the business leaders whose support he sought did not even
know where the two countries were located.

Yamashita managed to convince Taizo Ishizaka, the president
of Japan's Federation of Economic Organizations and the acknowledged leader of the Japanese business community, that
his cause was worthwhile. Ishizaka mobilized the Zaikai's support and turned Yamashita's project into a Zaikai project. Ishizaka literally allocated a share of the investment to each of Japan's major industries—utility companies, trading companies,
banks, steel firms, and the like. Many of them participated less
because of cold economic calculations than because they felt
obligated to support a national-interest project promoted by an
entrepreneur with the strong support of the Zaikai. Few even
dreamed that the project would soon provide Japan with a
highly profitable foothold in crude oil production in the Middle
East.

Yamashita was lucky. Within a year after his company was established, it discovered a rich field which later proved to be one
of the largest in the world, and in March 1961 the first shipment
arrived in Japan. By 1974 the flow of crude approached 400,000
barrels a day, making Arabian Oil one of the leading indepen-

dent producers in the world. Until the early 1970s the company was the only Japanese producer of crude oil and supplied nearly 10 percent of all the crude oil consumed in Japan.

From the beginning, the company's total output was slated to be exported to Japan for domestic consumption. Since the company had no downstream operations, however, it had to find outlets for its crude oil. Yamashita persuaded MITI that the development of Japanese-controlled crude supplies was so important that it should intercede on the company's behalf. Accordingly, MITI worked out an arrangement which subsequently became known as the pro rata formula. It called for the Japan Petroleum Association, the trade association of both foreign-owned and national refineries, to purchase the entire output of Arabian Oil and allocate it to each refinery according to its share of the total refining capacity.

Except for one or two very minor projects, there were no other entries to oil exploration until the late 1960s. This fact was a distinct departure from the normal pattern of Japanese business behavior. Typically, large Japanese companies competed vigorously to enter new fields, particularly when the first entrant was successful. Why did this not take place in oil? The Japanese industry still found the entry barriers too formidable.

The need to amass large amounts of capital was a major stumbling block. Few enterprises could match the unique way in which Yamashita had raised his capital. It was particularly significant that former Zaibatsu groups with the potential capacities of mobilizing a large sum of money failed to undertake large-scale entries at this time. Their reluctance lay largely in the lack of strong government support for oil ventures abroad. In the prewar era, Zaibatsu had entered some new but strategically important fields in actions which at first glance seemed rather daring. The holding company had a certain amount of risk money or venture capital to initiate new industries. On closer examination, however, it is clear that the Zaibatsu, particularly after the 1890s, had become rather cautious and entered new fields only with the assurance of strong government backing. Thus the postwar conservatism of the Zaibatsu system was partly only a perpetuation of a trait already ingrained.

Moreover, independent Zaibatsu firms were now pursuing their own growth programs in much familiar and less risky fields. Their banks were already having troubles fulfilling constant demand for funds from their major clients. The bank-centered groups were even less interested than the Zaibatsu in high-risk ventures requiring a large amount of capital.

Another barrier preventing the Japanese from entering into oil ventures abroad was their almost total lack of skill, understanding, or experience in dealing with foreign governments, particularly those of developing countries. Their own internal homogeneity and an absence in their history of continuing contacts with other cultures had prevented the Japanese from developing such capacities. The only entity often presumed to possess such skills were leading trading companies. In fact, however, during the period under consideration, they had yet to develop them despite their extensive foreign presence, since large-scale trading in standard products usually required neither a profound understanding of the society of a country nor extensive and difficult negotiations with its government. Japanese managers also lacked any thorough understanding of practices common in the international oil industry.

Even Yamashita made one serious error. Unfamiliar with the pattern commonly followed by large oil companies of incorporating each project as a subsidiary, he set up the Arabian Oil Company as both the investing and the operating entity. Since the two local governments had 20 percent ownership, this structure later hampered the company from operating freely and flexibly. The opposition of the two governments, for example, frustrated the desire of the Japanese management and stockholders to diversify into other geographic areas.

Not until the mid-1960s did MITI begin to formulate policies and programs to encourage private interests to explore and develop crude oil. In the eyes of MITI officials, the forces that led to the passage of the Petroleum Law in 1962 became even more pressing in subsequent years. In 1965 oil supplied nearly 60 percent of the country's total energy needs. The amount consumed was nearly double what it had been in 1960. Moreover, MITI's efforts to reduce the control of international companies at the refining stage had been faltering. In 1965 as much as two thirds of the nation's crude oil requirements were still purchased through captive relationships controlled by international oil companies either by means of ownership or long-term supply contracts negotiated as a result of debt obligations. It was apparent to MITI officials that in order to wrest control from foreign oil companies Japan had to seek her own sources of crude oil.

Japan was hardly unique in wanting to reduce her dependence

on foreign companies for a strategic product like oil. Other governments had already created national instruments for solving similar dilemmas. The British government, for example, had financed the expansions of the Anglo-Persian Oil Company to reduce the nation's dependence on U.S.-owned oil companies. The Compagnie Française des Petroles came into being for much the same reason.

In the Japanese case, however, there were certain elements rooted in the particular mentality nurtured by Japan's long history and tradition. Japan is a geographically isolated island nation; unlike Great Britain, she has a long history of economic and cultural isolation. Even prior to the two centuries of self-imposed and rigorously enforced isolation during the Tokugawa era (1600–1868), her location had prevented her from frequent and close interaction with other countries. In part because of this isolation, Japan developed as an extremely homogeneous society, tied by a common race, religion, and culture. As I noted earlier, the culture which thus evolved gave a great deal of emphasis to groups and very little to individuals. This strong group orientation and homogeneity tended to accentuate the uniqueness of the Japanese, not only in their own minds, but in those of foreigners.

A strong internal cohesiveness in groups at all levels helped breed a deep-seated suspicion in the Japanese against anyone outside the system. This feeling was evident in the dealings of the Japanese with other nations. This sense of isolation and suspicion was further reinforced by the history of Japan's industrialization. At several critical times in Japan's modern history, a coalition of Western powers had substantially frustrated Japan's growing interests in the world.

Even in the 1960s, the view was quite persistent among the Japanese elite that, in time of crisis, the United States and Western European countries, which for the most part arose from the same racial and cultural background, would form an alliance against Japan. Whether or not such a belief was relevant to the power politics of the 1960s was not important. What was critical was that it was widespread among Japan's policy planners.

Moreover, the Japanese had had a particularly bitter wartime experience with oil. An immediate impetus of Japan's involvement in World War II was the blockade of oil supplies to Japan imposed by the Allied countries in 1940. Japan entered the war with less than one year's supply of oil stockpiled. Under-standably, therefore, the initial Japanese military strategy placed top priority on securing petroleum resources in Southeast Asia.

The mid-1960s was also the time when MITI's concern over the invasion of large multinational enterprises was at its peak. The pressure for opening Japan to foreign capital had become all but irresistible; in fact, the capital liberalization program under con-sideration then had become dubbed popularly as the "second coming of the black ships." [5] MITI officials shared many of their concerns about multinational enterprises, the bureaucratic elites in other countries, but what they feared most was that multina-tional enterprises might be used as instruments to implement the national policies of their home governments.[6] Nurtured in the Japanese environment, such a possibility did not seem re-mote to MITI officials. For the reasons already noted, oil seemed particularly vulnerable.

Thus, by the mid-1960s forces were converging to heighten MITI's desire to search for crude oil sources owned, controlled, and managed by Japanese. By 1967 MITI's policy was clearly ar-ticulated. Though its terms were couched in terms of an entire national energy policy, oil was its central consideration. MITI es-tablished the so-called "30 percent self-sufficiency goal"; by 1985, in other words, it wanted 30 percent of Japan's crude oil requirement to be supplied by Japanese-controlled sources. To this end, the government committed itself to provide public funds to share the risks of exploration with Japanese private in-terests.

In 1967, to implement this new strategy, the government es-tablished the Japan Petroleum Development Corporation (JPDC), a wholly owned government corporation subject to MITI's policy guidance. In line with Japan's postwar industrial policy, the development of oil was to be left largely to private initiative; the role of the government was to assist private ef-forts, particularly in the exploration stages where risk was great-est. The JPDC was authorized to invest and loan money for over-seas exploration for oil and natural gas, to guarantee loans for such purposes, to give technical advice, and to conduct geologi-cal investigations. The form of the JPDC's financial participation in exploration projects was up to the private corporation in-volved. The maximum interest for its loans was 6.2 percent and repayment was to be forgiven if the project failed. The JPDC restricted its direct investments to the exploration phase and was required by law to divest itself of any equity interest once a project entered development stages.

Shortly after the clear articulation of MITI's policy and the establishment of the JPDC, a well-known Japanese phenomenon began. Leading companies began to scramble to get into oil exploration. By this time, an increasing number of Japanese companies had gained the capacity to overcome those intangible but serious barriers to entry into foreign countries including the ability to negotiate concession contracts with foreign governments and to plan and implement large-scale projects in remote areas of the world. Trading companies, particularly, had become involved in a large number of manufacturing investments and national development projects of various sorts in foreign countries—experiences which enhanced their ability to put together large-scale foreign ventures in which the host government had an important stake. Thus, from 1968 on, oil projects abroad proliferated (see Table 2-1), initiated by several sources.

The first was a group of large trading companies. To the major trading companies, particularly Zaibatsu-based ones, coal had been an important commodity because of the Zaibatsu's traditionally strong coalmining interests. As oil began to replace coal as the source of energy, however, trading companies began to shift their emphasis from coal to oil. In the late 1950s leading companies had begun to handle crude oil imports for some of the national companies. By the early 1960s chemicals and petrochemicals had become a key product for the large trading companies. And, finally, the trading companies saw opportunities in the field of oil to capitalize on their distinctive organizational capabilities.

A strong interest in oil exploration also began to be evident among major consumers of oil products such as electrical utilities and steel manufacturers—some of which had already jointly established small captive refineries—as well as among major manufacturers of petroleum-related products like synthetic fibers and petrochemicals.

The role of oil refineries in oil exploration has been fairly limited. At the end of 1973 oil refineries held less than 12 percent of the aggregate investment in all of the forty-two ventures then in existence. Nearly half of Japanese refining capacities were in the hands of foreign affiliates, which had already been integrated into a multinational system. The national refineries were highly fragmented and though fully cognizant of the advantages of vertical integration, only a few were able to amass sufficient resources.

The initial strategy followed by Japanese oil exploration companies had three major characteristics. With no prior experience to Japanese enterprises the first priority was the acquisition of knowledge. The knowledge to be gained ranged from technical and geological fields as well as to organizational skills and the ability to deal with various types of government. The desire to obtain knowledge and experience quickly pushed the Japanese oil exploration companies to scatter in wide geographic areas. With characteristic zeal, the Japanese sought out exploration rights in many parts of the world, and the forty-two projects in existence in 1973 were scattered all over the world, in the Middle East, Africa, Southeast Asia, North America, Latin America, and Oceania.

The second element in the initial strategy stemmed from the fact that the firms entering into oil exploration were all in industries characterized by oligopoly. Their oligopolistic nature subjected these firms to strong pressure to match their competitors' moves into new fields, since it put a premium on maintaining the competitive equilibrium among chief rivals.[7] The entry of one competitior into such an important new field as oil presented a major threat to that equilibrium. From the point of view of senior managers of a petrochemical company, for example, the discovery of a major oil field by one of its rivals was a serious threat. It might very well give the rival company decided advantages in raw material cost. The fact that the precise impact was difficult to measure beforehand only accentuated the threat. Even if the rival were not so fortunate as to strike oil on its first or second attempt, it would certainly gain new knowledge, which might be used to considerable advantage in subsequent projects. To protect themselves against such risks, utility firms, steel manufacturers, and trading companies followed the common oligopolistic strategy of competitive matching. In Japan, such pressures are even more intense, because various industrial and financial groups as well as individual companies are compelled to maintain an equilibrium.

The third element in the strategy involved sharing risks. Entry barriers were still high: enormous capital had to be amassed and Japan still had few trained and experienced technical people. Even more serious than these barriers was the intrinsic risk involved in oil exploration. To overcome these problems, Japanese oil exploration companies, like their predecessors in other countries, pursued a strategy of risk sharing through joint ventures. This arrangement enabled the companies engaged in oil exploration to pool their resources and also to divide whatever risk they took among a number of simultaneous exploration ventures. By forming joint ventures with rival companies, Japanese firms were able to minimize both the risks of exploration and the risks associated with the discovery of oil by rivals. Thus, all forty-two of the projects which had come into being by 1973 were joint ventures, often involving cross-holding of stock among major competitors. The four major trading companies, for example, were joint participants in sixteen projects, the four leading steel manufacturers in fifteen projects; and the five largest electric utility companies in ten projects.

In the early stages of development—shortly after the formation of the Japan Petroleum Development Corporation in 1967—the two uniquely Japanese institutions were the chief instruments for organizing oil exploration ventures. One was the Zaikai and the other was the trading company.

To put together joint ventures or consortia in oil exploration involving different companies required the intervention of an intermediary or promoter with considerable organizational skill to bring together different interests. The Zaikai leaders were uniquely suited to fill this role because of the special status accorded to them by the business community as a whole. Zaikai leaders were generally reluctant to become involved directly in any new industrial undertakings because their role prescribed that they be above such matters. Oil ventures, however, were different because of their importance to the nation. In a society governed by a tightly knit web of human relations, the status of a promoter or intermediary is a particularly critical factor in determining the amount of resources that could be mobilized to a project. The fact that some of them had come from the public utilities and steel industries helped them mobilize the resources of these industries. For these reasons, the Zaikai-sponsored projects organized in the late 1960s tended to have a large number of partners, often as many as twenty corporations drawn from several industries.

Major trading companies assumed an organization role for different reasons. Oil had, of course, become increasingly important to trading companies. In addition leading companies recognized the opportunities in oil exploration to capitalize on their unique organizational capacity for putting together large-scale foreign ventures. Though their own skills in this area were distinctly limited, they were nevertheless a definite advantage, since no other Japanese organization could match them. In oil projects, furthermore, they saw the possibility of large-scale sales of construction materials, machineries, and equipment. The projects organized by trading companies tended to be more narrowly based than those sponsored by Zaikai leaders, since trading companies generally confined themselves to soliciting the participation of companies which shared their own Zaibatsu or banking ties.

By the early 1970s, the strategy of Japanese oil exploration companies had begun to take on several new dimensions. For one thing, the initial strategy soon led to a large number of small fragmented ventures. This situation was exacerbated by the fact that Japanese antitrust law prohibited the holding company so that each project had to be organized as a separate operating entity. A number of exploration projects were quickly organized and poorly conceived. Many had difficulty mobilizing sufficient financial resources, particularly after their initial exploration efforts proved unsuccessful. Within two or three years, a number of such projects became dormant.

As problems of fragmentation became apparent, the first to pursue a strategy of consolidation were the Zaibatsu and banking groups. They recognized the advantages of consolidation and saw in the group an effective mechanism for achieving it. Indeed, the Zaibatsu and banking groups lent themselves well to large-scale, high-risk ventures like oil exploration. Clearly, such a group was in an excellent position to mobilize capital. Their trading company could cope with entry barriers external to Japan. Their chemical and petrochemical firms and oil refineries could provide outlets for crude oil. And their long traditions and shared understanding certainly facilitated communication.

The first to form a group-wide oil enterprise was Mitsui, which established the Mitsui Petroleum Development Corporation in 1969. In 1972 twenty-seven Mitsubishi enterprises formed Mitsubishi Petroleum Development Corporation. In 1973 the Sumitomo group followed suit. In the same year, oil companies were created by several major banking groups, including the Fuji Bank group, the Daichi Kangyo Bank group, and the Sanwa Bank group. Once again, the strategy of competitive matching was evident in the manner in which these group-based companies came into being. A firm could not legally serve exclusively as a holding company for a group's oil ventures, but it could hold equity in other oil ventures, as long as it had some direct operations of its own. Through this instrument, various groups began to achieve greater control and coordination among the oil ventures associated with them.

At the same time, the strategy of risk sharing was extended to joint ventures with foreign oil companies. Most of the earlier Japanese oil projects were undertaken exclusively by Japanese interests primarily because of the rather explicit policy of MITI, whose central objective was to reduce Japan's dependence on foreign oil companies. Despite MITI's sentiments however, Japanese companies found the barriers to entry into oil exploration were indeed formidable. By the time they came onto the world oil scene, the Japanese found that many of the attractive reserves and even exploration rights had been claimed already by large international companies. Often collaboration among domestic companies did not succeed in amassing sufficient capital. Although the technical skills and managerial know-how that the Japanese lacked were by this time available for hire in the United States and Europe, the peculiar nature of Japanese organization and management made it difficult for the Japanese to seek out these men and use them productively in a totally Japanese-managed organization. All these forces pushed Japanese companies into cooperative arrangements with large international oil companies. The latter, of course, had been watching Japanese moves carefully, for every new entry posed a potential threat to the stability of the industry.

For more than half a century, the maintenance of stability had been a major preoccupation of large oil companies, and they had resorted to a variety of means, including cartels, pricing conventions, and cooperative arrangements of various sorts.[8] Indeed, during this period the international giants had successfully tamed a number of new oil companies. By the end of the 1950s the maintenance of stability had become even more important to the large international companies, as the industry had begun to experience a steady decline in the barriers of entry.

In the 1950s, with the loss of cartels and the erosion of the effectiveness of the pricing conventions, cooperative arrangements at all levels of activities had become the dominant means of maintaining stability. One kind of arrangement was the joint producing subsidiary.[9] This helped to create a community of interest among potential rivals and tended to increase the probability of cooperation.

The sudden and aggressive entry of Japanese interests posed a special threat to the oil industry. Since they were so anxious to find attractive reserves quickly, the Japanese might well deviate significantly from conventional industry practices by offering extraordinarily favorable terms to exporting countries. It was also possible that they would upset the precariously maintained stability by finding new lower-cost supplies in unfamiliar locations. Thus the Japanese and the large international oil companies found that they had a common interest in cooperation. Twenty-three of the forty-two projects in existence in the summer of 1974 had foreign partners. These cooperative arrangements involved a number of companies in widely scattered locations, including Mobil in Zaire, Deminex in Peru, Continental off the coast of Thailand, and ERAP in Iraq, Getty in Peru, Exxon in Indonesia, British Petroleum and the Compagnie des Pétroles in Abu Dhabi.

The third dimension in the strategy emerging in the early 1970s was the pursuit of vertical integration. Practically all the oil exploration projects began without a direct link with downstream operations. Only a handful initiated by refineries had had built-in opportunities for integration from the start. Vertical integration—self-sufficiency within the enterprise for production, refining, transportation, and marketing—had become an important element in the strategy of the world oil industry.

Such a strategy had become apparent among large international oil companies by the turn of the century.[10] A handful of U.S. and European companies first competed in the export market at the marketing level, largely because U.S. oil companies had developed a distinct strength in marketing at home and were eager to use it to penetrate export markets. They soon realized that because of the relative ease of entry, competitors could not be contained at the marketing level. This realization pushed oil companies to seek to erect entry barriers by controlling crude supply. This led to a fundamental shift in their strategy, and they began to search for vertical integration.[11]

The pressure for vertical integration was fed by two closely related features of the oil industry. Primarily because of high fixed costs, the economy of scale is extremely important at every stage of operations in the oil industry, particularly in the production of crude oil. Stemming from these high fixed costs is the oligopolistic structure of the industry. A handful of large oil companies recognized that they had to find means other than price to stabilize their production and sales. In an oligopolistic industry a price cut by one firm would simply elicit a similar response from its competitors, thereby defeating its purpose. Deprived of the use of price as an adjusting mechanism, oil companies turned to developing captive refining and marketing facilities to serve as outlets for their crude oil and to developing an internal capacity to stabilize production and sales.

Vertical integration by producers of crude oil posed a serious threat to firms still specializing in refining or marketing, compelling them to take similar action to reduce their vulnerability against vertically integrated producers. Because suppliers were limited, nonintegrated companies would have to purchase their crude supplies from integrated producers, who would be in a position to charge monopolistic prices to drive them out of business. Similar forces pushed Japanese oil-producing companies to the strategy of vertical integration.

In the summer of 1974 only four of the Japanese oil projects were producing and none was fully vertically integrated, but the strategy for vertical integration was in motion. Several different structural patterns were beginning to emerge. One was vertical integration within a Zaibatsu or banking group. Though Zaibatsu and major banking groups had lacked strong ties to the oil refining business, some links had been forged during the 1960s. This took several forms. First, petrochemical firms—usually core members in Zaibatsu or banking groups—built small captive refineries. Second, through credit extension, most of the Zaibatsu and other major banks had established connections with the Japanese-owned refineries known as national companies.

Capitalizing on these relationships, the Zaibatsu and bank-centered groups began to achieve at least a semblance of vertical integration within the group. It would be highly unlikely in the Japanese tradition, for a group's oil company to take any immediate or drastic actions vis-à-vis these refineries, such as outright acquisition. It is much more probable that before any drastic formal change in ownership is made, the group's oil company and its refineries will gradually build their mutual interests through a variety of means including limited cross-holding of stocks, long-term supply contracts, and interlocking of directorates. In some cases, the process of integration may actually stop short of any change in ownership, the parties involved settling for de facto integration, like that of the Keiretsu.

Trading companies also provided structures for vertical integration. Several major trading companies, notably C. Itoh, Mitsui, and Marubeni, had acquired an interest in small refineries to link up with the oil-producing companies of their own or with those belonging to their groups. Though their control over both crude and refining stages was only partial in almost all cases, trading companies began to see an opportunity to play their familiar integrative role in the oil industry—a role not unlike that of the traditional Keiretsu ties.

Another way for Japanese oil-producing companies to pursue the strategy of vertical integration would be to build refineries outside Japan. Given the already fragmented character of the refining industry in Japan, it would be virtually impossible to obtain MITI's approval for a new refinery there. Even if MITI approval were obtained, finding suitable sites would pose enormous problems. Any plan to build a refinery was likely to encounter severe opposition from the local community. To solve these problems would require time-consuming and difficult negotiations. Thus, the prospect of establishing refineries outside Japan was particularly attractive to companies which lacked ties to downstream operations in Japan.

Although no such projects had yet been realized in the summer of 1974, several were under serious consideration. For example, C. Itoh had signed an agreement to build a 200,000-barrel-a-day refinery in Singapore jointly with AMOCO and the government of Singapore. The agreement called for AMOCO to supply crude oil and C. Itoh to assume responsibility for distributing half of the refined output. Arabian Oil was considering a refinery in Malaysia with British Petroleum and Caltex.

Teijin, a synthetic fiber manufacturer which had begun to take on new functions, planned to establish a major refinery in Korea jointly with local interests. Teijin planned to supply the crude oil from its Iranian and Nigerian reserves, once those fields began production. Reportedly, the National Iranian Oil Company, Teijin's partner in crude oil production in Iran, was also to participate in this venture. Two Japanese trading companies (Mitsubishi and Nissho-Iwai), along with three refining firms (Daikyo, Maruzen, and Mitsubishi Oil), were exploring the idea of building a refinery in Indonesia jointly with Pertermina, Indonesia's state-owned oil company.

The third strategy emerging in the mid-1970s was that of multinationalization, another distinctive feature of the world oil industry.[12] The multinationalization of the oil industry came about
as a direct result of its strategy of vertical integration. As long as
U.S. and European oil companies concentrated on marketing activities, the price of crude oil was not an important consideration. They simply sought out the cheapest sources. But as each
company began to seek vertical integration, it began to pay the
closest attention to the price levels of crude oil, because if its
competitors should gain access to sources cheaper than its own,
its position and indeed the stability of the whole industry would
be threatened. Moreover, well-diversified crude sources in
various parts of the world would provide insurance against
supply blockage. For these reasons, oil companies began to pursue a policy of participating in the exploration of any new major
areas. Thus, in the early decades of this century, U.S. and European oil companies took on a multinational character.

The original goal of Japanese oil exploration projects was
clearly that of supplying the needs of the Japanese market. By
the early 1970s, however, there were growing signs that Japanese oil firms had begun to deviate from that overriding commitment and to take on a multinational character. Arabian Oil Company, for example, Japan's first and major oil company, had
begun to sell as much as one third of its output to the majors.
The company had no captive refinery. The refineries in Japan,
foreign as well as national, had for some time resented the so-
called pro rata formula imposed by MITI, whereby they were
compelled to buy the crude oil produced by Arabian Oil. By the
late 1960s, the high sulfur content of the company's crude oil
posed an even more serious marketing problem in Japan. Compelled to seek other outlets, Arabian Oil turned to the international companies. By 1970 it had launched active programs to
diversify its markets and entered into long-term supply contracts
with several international companies. The company's move in
1973 to build a refinery in Malaysia jointly with British Petroleum
and Caltex was another step in this direction.

The establishment of refineries outside Japan, although it may
be motivated chiefly by a desire for vertical integration, is likely
to push the Japanese firms to pursue a multinational strategy. Although the companies' initial intention may be to supply the Japanese market, once these foreign refineries are established, and
the companies' crude oil production increases as well, the high

fixed costs associated with production and refining will put powerful pressure on the companies to increase their refining capacity, and this in turn will encourage them to expand their outlets beyond Japan.

The Role of Government

One important way in which the structure of Japan's oil exploration program departed from the ones developed earlier in Great Britain, France, and Italy was in the role of the government. In all four instances, government played an important role in initiating and promoting national efforts to enter the oil industry, but their styles differed. The Japanese structure reflected its traditional business and government relationship.

In encouraging development of Japan's crude oil sources, the government took the initiative, committing itself to share risks with private interests. As it had done in a number of other instances the government singled out oil as a high priority industry and proceeded to formulate goals and plans for it. This action had implications far beyond any tangible financial support government might provide. It gave a legitimacy to oil exploration, thereby helping to eliminate the personal risk of promoting oil projects. Previously, any professional manager contemplating an entry into oil had to weigh the possible impact on his career and reputation of becoming involved in such a high-risk venture.

Because of the high risk involved and the importance of oil, MITI created a special institution, the Japan Petroleum Development Corporation. The JPDC, however, was not a national oil company in the mold of B.P., or C.F.P. Rather, its main function was that of providing capital to encourage private institutions to undertake risky ventures. Its role was strictly confined to the exploration stage and precluded any managerial power at all in the companies that received investment or loans. At the end of 1973 the JPDC had investments ranging from 10 to 75 percent in twenty-four of the forty-two exploration companies.

In the mid-1970s MITI and JPDC were becoming increasingly interested in playing a more direct role in oil, because of its strategic value. The energy crisis of 1973–74 heightened this concern and led to various proposals to expand the role of MITI and particularly that of JPDC. Such proposals ranged from expanding the JPDC's financing functions to include the development stage, to enhancing the JPDC's management power over private oil companies, to transforming it into a giant national oil company. A prospect that these proposals will be implemented seem dim, however, at least in the mid-1970s. It would probably encounter active resistance from the business community which has begun to recognize oil as a highly profitable new area. Various powerful business groups have already gained a foothold in the industry, and the bureaucracy, though quite powerful in dealing with a single industry, stands little chance of overcoming strong objections by the leaders from the Zaikai and various Zaibatsu and banking groups.

Furthermore, despite its seemingly smooth relationship with government, the business community fosters a deep-seated suspicion that government enterprise is inefficient. Few government-owned monopolies have been successful in Japan. The largest and the best-known public enterprise is National Railroad System, and despite its high technical efficiency, its management had been notoriously ineffective.

The business community would also object to increasing managerial power of the JPDC because it would mean an erosion of their power and because of the manner in which the JPDC's managerial perogatives were likely to be exercised. If JPDC's role were expanded, it would become much more assertive in the management of those companies in which it had investment or loans. Particularly, the business community fears that MITI and JPDC would pressure oil-producing companies to appoint retired government bureaucrats to top management positions, a practice that has been fairly common in Japan. There is an informal understanding in the Japanese bureaucracy that senior career bureaucrats must retire from civil service in their early fifties, and most of these men seek a second career in business or politics. The bureaucracy has developed a rather subtle but highly effective system of placing these men in appropriate positions in private firms. Its main targets, of course, are companies with close government ties. In some industries, the practice has become so routine that certain positions are reserved for these men. This process is popularly known as *Amakadori,* which literally means "descending from heaven," a phrase poignantly suggestive of certain aspects of the relationship between government and business in Japan.

The practice is deeply resented by industry. It distinctly limits the career opportunities of men who spend their entire lives in a company. The talents of the retired bureaucrats vary. Some go on to become outstanding executives, but others find it difficult to adjust to the change. Once a man is hired, however, the company is morally obliged to retain him for at least ten years. Many business leaders feel that this is the worst form of government participation in private enterprise.

In the mid-1970s these objections carried particular weight, since MITI found itself in a weaker and weaker position vis-à-vis private industry. Several forces were responsible for this changing climate—some specific to the industry and others related to the broader environment. The increasing multinationalization of the Japanese oil industry was important in two ways. In the mid-1970s Japanese enterprises have acquired the capacity to achieve vertical integration completely outside Japan—a potential unthinkable even in the late 1960s and one which challenges the basic premise of the Petroleum Law of 1962. For MITI to apply the Petroleum Law to Japanese-owned refineries abroad, particularly when they were jointly owned by foreign interests, would raise the familiar and thorny problems involved in the extraterritorial application of national regulations.

As Japanese oil firms increased their interdependence with multinational enterprises and their sophistication about them, they began to question the fairly simplistic notion of multinational enterprises, widely shared by MITI officials. By the mid-1970s MITI was no longer able to stir and rally business interests to the ministry's goals by appealing to a naive fear of multinational enterprises. In fact, Japan's oil interests were becoming increasingly uncomfortable about MITI's nationalistic rhetoric. Under pressure from the industry, MITI was beginning to soften its nationalistic stance and to stress international cooperation.

The oil crisis further weakened MITI's ability to control the Japanese oil business. MITI, like the governments of other major oil consuming nations, was helpless in influencing the allocation of oil during the period of crisis. The allocation of petroleum was taken over by the major multinational oil companies. Furthermore, they did not behave in concert as MITI had predicted they might under such circumstances. MITI had supposed that the multinational oil companies would give the overriding priority to their respective home countries, bowing to policy directives from Washington, London, or Paris. MITI expected them to act in unison against Japan, because of Japan's long-standing discrimination against them.

When the crisis came, however, the multinational oil companies did not act in unison. Each, pursuing its own self-interest, behaved in its own manner. B.P. and C.F.P. acted as MITI had predicted, cutting their supplies to Japan almost entirely. Because of repeated rebuffs from MITI, these companies had no affiliates in Japan and commanded only a marginal market position.

In contrast, Caltex, Mobil, Exxon and Shell each had an affiliate of its own and an important stake in the Japanese market. Their strategy was clear. They saw a unique opportunity to strengthen the market position of their respective affiliates in a highly competitive market by undermining their competitors, particularly the national companies. Thus, they drastically reduced or even eliminated their shipment to national companies but continued to supply their affiliates on favorable terms. The behavior of each multinational enterprise was determined primarily by what it perceived as its business interest, irrespective of the wishes of its home government.

Fundamental changes in the environment contributed even more forcefully to the declining influence of MITI and the JPDC on the future course of Japanese oil policy. Throughout the 1950s, and 1960s, MITI's overriding commitment was to build modern industries in Japan and develop them into the most competitive in the world. Its objectives were clear, and so were its priorities. MITI's excellent, idealistic, yet pragmatic bureaucrats were single-mindedly committed to them. The prestige and morale of the ministry were high, and it was able to stir and rally private industry around a national purpose. As the champion of economic growth and the guardian of Japan's national interest, it enjoyed such strong public support that it was frequently able to overpower other ministries and agencies, including the rather feeble Fair Trade Commission, in helping businesses achieve rationalization through joint planning, cooperation in capital investment, and consolidation. The ministry's control over the import of goods and technology and the inflow of foreign capital and its ability to dispense subsidies were particularly strong sources of power.

All this had changed by the early 1970s. MITI was facing a new environment, one much less sympathetic and supportive of its goals and ideology than that of the 1960s. The national consensus that economic growth should be the nation's overriding goal had eroded, and the public was growing increasingly concerned over the serious deterioration of the environment resulting directly from MITI's intense promotion of heavy industry. Consumers were so stirred that they began to protect their interests in an organized manner, subjecting big business to serious public attack. Meantime, MITI had lost much of its control over import of goods and technology and entry of foreign capital. Besides, no major industries remained in need of promotion. MITI's role changed from that of promoter of private business interests to that of regulator. It found itself enforcing antipollution regulations, anti-inflationary price controls, and consumer protection laws. MITI's officials argue that their involvement in these programs is in the best long-term interests of Japanese industry, but business has reacted to controls with something less than enthusiasm. One reflection of the change in national mood is the fact that, by the mid-1970s, MITI was no longer in a position to intercede effectively on behalf of private enterprises against the Fair Trade Commission. An illustration of this took place in the spring of 1974. For example, when the F.T.C. indicted a number of Japanese oil refining firms for price fixing from 1970 to 1973, it publicly accused MITI of facilitating an administrative cartel among certain oil refineries.

Against such a background, in the mid-1970s it became highly unlikely that MITI would be able to transform the Japan Petroleum Development Corporation into a central organization to control and coordinate Japanese oil ventures abroad. The government's role will most likely be confined to sharing risks in the exploration stage and to providing a part of the enormous capital required at the development stage. Its role in management is likely to be narrowly prescribed.

How unique is the Japanese experience in foreign ventures in oil? Advanced nations, notably Great Britain, France, and Italy had developed their national oil companies. A comparison with similar efforts elsewhere will illuminate the Japanese pattern. The experience of B.P., C.F.P., and E.N.I., though much earlier than that of Japan, had three features in common.[13] First, each was established in order to provide a nation with some degree of independence from foreign oil companies. For example, the major motive for investing in British Petroleum in 1914 was to reduce Great Britain's dependence on American oil. C.F.P. came into being a decade later, for basically the same reason. Italy's E.N.I organized after World War II, was explicitly committed to the goal of establishing Italian independence from large international oil companies.

The second feature the three have in common is direct government ownership, though its forms and degree differ. The

British government owns 48.9 percent of B.P.; the French government holds a 25 percent interest in C.F.P.; E.N.I. is a 100 percent government-owned holding company, although the management of its operating subsidiaries is apparently given a great deal of autonomy.

Third, despite their initial goal of independence, in the course of their development all three companies had become hardly distinguishable in their strategies from one another as well as from other major oil companies. In fact, B.P. had become one of the largest of the so-called seven majors. C.F.P., though somewhat late in its development had become firmly committed to the strategies of vertical integration and multinational operations. It has built an extensive network of marketing activities in other European countries, Africa, Australia, and even the United States. The company has also entered extensive cooperative arrangements with other oil companies.

The transformation of E.N.I.'s strategy was even more remarkable because its founder, Enrico Mattei, intensely disliked the majors and persistently sought to take an independent course. Shortly after his death, however, in the early 1960s, E.N.I. too made a drastic shift in its strategy. By 1965 E.N.I.'s interest had become sufficiently intertwined with that of other companies that an editor of a trade journal sympathetic to the majors and long critical of E.N.I.'s attitude toward them stated that "the erstwhile rebel is responding to the realities of the international oil business." [14]

Japanese entry into the exploration and development of crude oil abroad began in a unique way, initiated by an entrepreneur who was a total stranger to the oil industry. The motives of those who participated were a peculiar combination of pecuniary desires and patriotism, a common one in Japan's industrial history. The government played its traditional role of initiator, promoter, and consensus builder, but the initiative was left to the private sector. Unlike any of the three European countries, the Japanese government did not create a national oil company.

Soon after the Japanese oil projects got under way, however, the process of convergence became noticeable in their strategies in response to the same forces that have shaped the development of the international oil industry for nearly a century. What was remarkable was the speed with which the Japanese industry began to make the shift. Yet in implementing the strategies of vertical integration, risk sharing, and multinationalization, Japanese oil interests relied on uniquely Japanese institutions like Zaibatsu, banking groups, trading companies, and even Keiretsu. The Zaikai had a role to play as intermediaries and promoters. In its structure, the Japanese oil projects would most likely maintain distinctively Japanese elements.

Table 2-1. Emergence of companies engaged in oil exploration outside Japan, 1965–73

FISCAL YEAR	NUMBER OF NEW COMPANIES FORMED	AMOUNT OF INVESTMENT (¥ MILLION)
1965 or earlier	3	83,552
1966	3	11,429
1967	1	11,834
1968	2	21,336
1969	5	26,697
1970	6	35,614
1971	8	43,401
1972	5	113,558
1973	9	200,000[a]
Total	42	547,429

Source: Adapted from *Sekyu shiryo, 1973* (Petroleum statistics, 1973; Tokyo: Ministry of International Trade and Industry, 1974), pp. 94–96.

[a] Estimate.

3. The Spread of Manufacturing

In raw material ventures, as illustrated by oil, the strategies of Japanese multinational enterprises have become firmly committed to the road toward convergence. Have similar historical parallels been taking place in the manufacturing industries? As a first step toward answering this central question, let us begin with a brief comparison in the patterns of multinational spread of American and Japanese manufacturing industries.

Such a comparison reveals several striking differences. One of the most dramatic is a difference in the size of the countries' respective investments. At the end of fiscal year 1972, the total of Japanese investment stood at around $1.75 billion in contrast to a total for the United States of over $39 billion. In other words, Japan had invested a total of only 4 percent of that of the United States.

The types of industries that have become multinational in the two countries also differ. American manufacturing activities abroad have been dominated by large diversified enterprises which place heavy emphasis on capital and skilled manpower.[1] Among the industries in which multinationalization has been most extensive are those involved in petroleum refining and the manufacture of motor vehicles, drugs, and other chemicals. Among those in which it has been least active are the textile and steel industries. In Japan the situation is just the reverse; indeed textiles are in the forefront and account for nearly a quarter of the nation's total manufacturing investment. (See Table 3-1.)

A third distinct difference involves the location of foreign investment. Over 70 percent of Japanese manufacturing investment has been made in developing countries, and 60 percent of this amount has been concentrated in Asia. In contrast, over 80 percent of the U.S. foreign manufacturing investment has taken place in developed countries, most of it in Europe and Canada.

It is much easier to give a statistical description of the distinct features of the foreign manufacturing investment of two countries than to explain those differences. The pattern of development followed by U.S. multinational enterprises was shaped largely by the characteristics of the domestic economy.[2] During much of the past century, U.S. businessmen were exposed to unique stimuli—huge land and rich natural resources and a relative scarcity in labor. Although production skills of American labor were not high, the combination of rich natural resources and a high level of general education enabled the nation to attain a rapid increase in productivity throughout much of the nineteenth century—an increase that resulted in a high per capita income. This high standard of living created large and rather distinctive internal demands to which U.S. entrepreneurs responded by producing products uniquely suited to a high-income market and an economy characterized by a scarcity of labor. In the process American enterprises developed unique methods of mass production and marketing for their innovative products.

When Europe began to catch up in the 1870s, similar demands emerged there, triggering a rapid growth in the export of these products from the United States. In response Europe began to develop its own innovations as well as imitations, thereby threatening the export position of American companies. As the products matured, cost became an important consideration, and to counteract the threat American enterprises began to move their production facilities abroad to exploit what remained of their competitive advantage.

These firms, whose competitive advantage lay primarily in innovative technologies, were soon followed by firms which had developed, in America's unique environment, unusual skill in the mass production and mass marketing of standardized products through the active promotion of a trade name. Coca Cola, Corn Products, and General Foods for example, derived their chief oligopolistic advantage from product differentiation.

It is estimated that, by the turn of the century, there were already between 75 and 100 subsidiaries of American firms engaged in manufacturing activities abroad. By the end of the 1920s, 187 major U.S. multinational enterprises had established 467 manufacturing subsidiaries abroad, and by 1940 the number had increased to 715.

The pattern of Japanese industrial development was markedly different from that of the United States. When the process of catching up began in earnest in the early 1950s, partly because of MITI's policy, clusters of industries developed in sequence; in the mid-1950s textiles and steel; in the late 1950s, shipbuilding, electrical and nonelectrical machineries, and petroleum refining; in the early 1960s chemicals, consumer electronics, home appliances, and automobiles. And finally, in the mid-1960s petrochemicals gained momentum and serious efforts at developing the computer industry began. Unlike their U.S. counterparts, Japanese industries were technological followers, and most of the industries started in Japan in the 1950s and 1960s had already reached the mature stage in the United States. These industries once initiated, however, grew very rapidly in Japan. Within a decade, led by the phenomenal growth in the internal market, almost all of them had attained a productive capacity second only to that of the United States.

As the Japanese government and industry relentlessly pursued a strategy of building heavy industries, the domestic demand for steel, machineries, petroleum, and chemicals increased rapidly. Extensive postwar reforms, touching almost every aspect of Japanese life, helped spread the benefits of economic growth among the masses, and by the early 1960s a large mass market began to emerge. The rapidly growing mass market stimulated a surge in the manufacture of textiles, consumer electronics, home appliances, and then automobiles.[3]

The champions of the postwar industries—among them steel, chemicals, and automobiles were capital-intensive industries in which the economy of scale was critically important. The growth of domestic demand enabled them to attain sufficient scale to compete in the world market in the first place, and then their competitive ability was given a further boost by the rapid growth in export. Postwar technological advances made it possible to extend the economy of scale to other areas other than production. For example, giant ships specifically designed for transport of raw materials like iron ore and petroleum and finished products like automobiles benefited Japanese industries immensely.

The overriding importance of scale as a source of international competitive ability is evident in several Japanese industries. Let us first consider the case of the steel industry.[4] The industry began its postwar surge on a modest scale in the late 1940s. In 1955 the total output was still no more than 10 million tons, less than that of the United States, the Soviet Union, West Germany, or France. Subsequently, however, Japan's capacity doubled every five years. In 1965 the Japanese output exceeded 41,000 tons, more than that of France and West Germany. By the early 1960s the Japanese steel industry had become competitive in the export market, and between 1962 and 1966 the export grew an average of 40 percent per annum. Between 1966 and 1971, although the growth rate tapered off, it still averaged over 13 percent per annum.

In addition to economy of scale in production, the Japanese steel industry enjoyed other advantages. Major technological breakthroughs in shipbuilding made possible economies of scale in the transportation of ore. Furthermore, because of its heavy dependence on imported ore, the industry built its mills in areas that were directly accessible by ships. In contrast, in the United States and Germany, mills had been located inland close to domestic ore reserves, and when these reserves were depleted, these countries found themselves at a considerable disadvantage. Moreover, the very fact that almost all the Japanese steel mills had to be totally rebuilt after the war gave the industry unique opportunities to adopt the latest technologies on a large scale.

Another industry which grew in the postwar decades, from a very modest size to the second largest in the world was the synthetic fiber industry.[5] This industry began in 1951 when Toray introduced nylon under the license of DuPont. Teijin, another textile firm, soon followed Toray's lead with polyester fiber. In response to a booming domestic market, the synthetic fiber industry grew, expanding its output to 54,000 tons in 1955, to 210,000 tons in 1962, and to 380,000 tons in 1965. By 1970 the industry's capacity was the second highest in the world. The industry's export also grew rapidly; in 1958 export accounted for only about 5 percent of the total output of the industry; in 1962 it accounted for 17 percent; and by 1965 it had leaped ahead to account for at least a third of the total output.

A similar pattern was repeated in the home appliance and automobile industries. The home appliance and consumer electronics industry began to take off in 1955 as a mass consumer market began to emerge in Japan.[6] Between 1955 and 1960 the industry showed an average annual growth rate of 60 percent, mainly on the strength of electric fans, transistor radios, refrigerators, washing machines, and black-and-white television sets. The growth rate tapered off to about 10 percent per annum during the subsequent five years. Between 1966 and 1970 the introduction of color television sets gave another major boost to the industry. Export has grown steadily in importance. In 1957 it accounted for less than 5 percent of the total output; by 1962 it had increased to 11 percent; and by 1967 to 18 percent. In 1972 export accounted for more than 22 percent of the total output. The export of consumer electronics products has been particularly impressive, increasing from ¥7.2 billion in 1955 to ¥940 billion in 1972.

The Japanese automobile industry began on a modest scale in the 1930s primarily to satisfy military needs.[7] By 1951 the industry's capacity had reached 100,000 units, twice its prewar peak. In 1963 the output reached one million units. The industry did not really take off, however, until the mid-1960s when the domestic demand for passenger cars increased rapidly. Output doubled between 1963 and 1966, reaching 2 million units; in 1968 it was 3 million; and by 1970, 5 million. By 1968, in terms of capacity, the Japanese industry had become second only to that of the United States.

The automobile industry is a classic example of rapid growth stimulated by an expansion in domestic demands, particularly by individual consumers. Whereas in 1960 less than 8 percent of the passenger cars produced were purchased by individuals, by 1970 the share had increased 50 percent, and over 60 percent of the total number of automobiles produced were passenger cars. The rapid expansion of the domestic market in the mid-1960s enabled the Japanese automobile industry to become one of the most competitive in the world market. In 1960 the total number of motor vehicles exported from Japan was only 21,000. By 1965 it had reached 41,000. And within the subsequent seven years, the number of units exported was multiplied by 25.

Throughout the 1950s and much of the 1960s Japanese industries enjoyed certain additional advantages. They had an abundant supply of well-educated, well-disciplined, low-wage labor to draw on. They had ready access to foreign technologies. They benefited from a distinctly Japanese capacity to adopt foreign technologies to fit their own needs and the nation's factor endowments. In a number of industries, the Japanese were able to make significant improvements on the technologies they obtained from foreign sources. Japanese industries also had the advantage of active government export incentives in the forms of subsidies and low-interest credit. The trading companies were also a major help, at least for certain types of industries, such as steel and synthetic fiber. The trading companies with their worldwide networks and wide diversity of products were able to enjoy an economy of scale in distribution, making it possible for Japanese manufacturers to penetrate even relatively small markets.

Investment in Developing Countries

As some of the Japanese manufacturing industries became actively involved in export, they began to experience problems of import substitution in a number of developing countries. Aspirations to industrialize were certainly not new in these countries. In a few countries, like Japan, efforts to industrialize began before the turn of the century. The desire for industrialization accelerated among developing countries in the postwar decades. Almost all of them resorted to the familiar technique of restricting or even prohibiting the import of certain target products and of offering a variety of encouragements to induce the manufacture of these products domestically.

The target products are generally selected primarily on the basis of the size of the local market and of the local availability of the various inputs necessary. Cost was usually considered to be of secondary importance. Thus the manufacturing processes most likely to be singled out were those which produced consumer products, particularly the last stages of manufacturing or assembly, which can be performed on a limited scale. Japanese manufacturing industries in the early 1960s were particularly vulnerable on two accounts. For one thing, standard items, such as fabricated steel products, simple consumer durables, and textiles, contributed heavily to their export. Second, developing countries, particularly in Southeast Asia, were the most important markets for Japanese manufactured products. In the early 1960s, for example, 35 percent of the Japanese steel export, 42 percent of textiles, and 44 percent of consumer electronics and home appliances went to Southeast Asia. This concentration of Japanese export is not surprising. Not only is the area close to Japan geographically, but it is also the market Japan dominated in the prewar era and one in which lower-priced Japanese products had a special appeal. The desire to protect the export market was the primary force which galvanized Japanese firms to undertake local production. Of course, they were almost always aided by the incentives and protections offered by local governments.

The very recent origin of foreign manufacturing activities by Japanese firms is due to the fact that it was not until the late 1950s that export began to become important in a few Japanese industries. A good many others did not become competitive in the export market until the early 1960s. For example, among the subsidiaries established between 1951 and 1970 by the 43 Japanese manufacturing firms in the Fortune's list of the 200 largest non-U.S. companies, 208—over 56 percent—came into being only after 1965.

The geographical locations and products in which foreign manufacturing investment had taken place also reflected the pattern of Japanese export. (See Table 3-2 for breakdowns by geographic spreads; Table 3-3 for breakdowns by product lines.) Of the 367 manufacturing firms of the Fortune's 43 manufacturing companies for which the locations were known, over 62 percent were in Asia. Among the 249 subsidiaries for which data on product lines were available, over 60 percent were producing textiles, apparel, electric machinery, and fabricated metal, all of which had been among the major Japanese exports for some years.

Once a Japanese manufacturing firm took a plunge into foreign manufacturing, its decision stimulated similar behavior on the part of its rivals within the industry.[8] By the early 1960s Japanese export had come to be dominated by oligopolistic industries. Thus, any decision by a firm to establish a manufacturing subsidiary was seen by its rivals as a threat to the equilibrium of the industry maintained at the export stage—a threat which could only be met by matching actions. Such an investment was typically viewed as a means to perpetuate export from a firm's production facilities in Japan albeit in different forms. Manufacturers of home appliances, for example, could maintain their export of parts and components by creating small captive assembly facilities in a foreign market. Similarly, steel or synthetic fiber manufacturers could continue to export intermediate materials to foreign plants.

To manufacturers in capital-intensive industries where the economy of scale in production is vitally important, export had become a built-in element in capacity planning and utilization. The high fixed costs associated with such operations and certain additional elements of rigidity in the cost structure peculiar to

Japan made it vitally important for these enterprises to defend even the smallest export market. Matching behavior was further reinforced by the local government, for when imports were prohibited, prices were allowed to rise in the local market. This made it possible for investing companies to achieve a satisfactory profit from operations with much smaller scale than it could under normal conditions. In the light of these forces, it is hardly surprising to discover the rather close timing of the investments made in key Southeast Asian markets by the leading firms in the three industries which dominated Japanese manufacturing investments. (See Table 3-4.)

Anxious to capitalize on the economy of scale in production in Japan, the initial strategy pursued by Japanese firms in their foreign manufacturing activities usually called for maximizing export from Japanese plants and minimizing the value added by the foreign subsidiaries insofar as this was consistent with the requirements of the local government. A heavy reliance of Japanese foreign subsidiaries on the parent companies for supplies of intermediate materials, parts, and components were well illustrated by an extensive survey conducted by MITI among a random sample of 339 manufacturing firms with 661 foreign manufacturing subsidiaries.[9] According to this survey, in 1973 textile subsidiaries purchased about half of their raw materials from the Japanese parent companies; steel subsidiaries, 60 percent; consumer electronics subsidiaries nearly 67 percent; and subsidiaries manufacturing precision instruments and automobiles, an average of 77 to 82 percent.

A combination of three forces, namely the strategy of maximizing export from parent companies, the small size of the markets involved, and the crowding-in phenomenon caused by matching behavior limited the average size of Japanese manufacturing subsidiaries. This was particularly pronounced in Asia. (See Table 3-5.) The limited size of the Japanese manufacturing subsidiaries abroad is further confirmed by the sales data collected from the 222 of the 370 subsidiaries owned by the Fortune's 43 manufacturing companies. (See Table 3-6.)

The fact that the overseas subsidiaries are small should not be construed to mean that they are in aggregate unimportant in their host countries. In a few countries, they have already become dominant in certain industries because of the relatively small size of the market and the heavy concentration of Japanese subsidiaries. In Thailand, for example, in 1973 the aggregate of

Japanese subsidiaries were responsible for producing about 60 percent of all the textiles produced, 70 percent of consumer electronics and home appliances, and 80 percent of the automobiles.

The Japanese Advantages

In view of the fact that Japanese manufacturing investments abroad had been made mostly by mature industries, what competitive advantages did the Japanese enjoy over their local competitors, particularly over multinational enterprises of other national origins? The Japanese, unlike the Americans, could hardly compete on the basis of innovative technologies. Japanese manufacturers, however, particularly those who make intermediate materials like steel and synthetic fiber, did have a unique advantage in the Keiretsu, that network of small independent manufacturing firms loosely organized by a large trading company or manufacturing firm to complement one another's skills in performing a variety of specialized manufacturing and distribution functions.

The synthetic fiber industry made particularly good use of the Keiretsu, first in the domestic market and then in its ventures abroad. The two firms which pioneered the production of synthetic fiber in the early 1950s experienced serious difficulty marketing the new products. One of the main obstacles was the reluctance of firms engaged in spinning, weaving, dyeing, and apparel manufacturing to use synthetic fiber materials. Almost all these firms were small family-owned enterprises. Unsure what the response of the market would be, and lacking technical expertise, they were understandably reluctant to experiment with the new fibers. The fiber manufacturers had origins in the textile field and understood the concerns of these small firms. They saw that they could benefit by organizing a network of select groups of small firms into a Keiretsu pattern similar to that developed earlier in cotton textiles by trading companies, primarily for purposes of facilitating export. In building the Keiretsu relationship, the fiber manufacturers collaborated closely with major trading companies. The fiber manufacturers gave technical and managerial assistance to their respective Keiretsu enterprises; the trading companies took over the physical movement of goods among various Keiretsu firms and, at every point, extended credit to them.

The manufacturing firms also worked extensively on market

development through mass advertising and promotion. With the help of the trading companies, they built a Keiretsu network among wholesalers and distributors to push the new products through market channels. In this manner, with the aid of the trading companies fiber manufacturers achieved de facto vertical integration and built a unique system-based oligopoly. The Keiretsu provided the two pioneering firms with an effective, albeit temporary, entry barrier.

The trading companies performed export functions for the synthetic fiber industry, much as they had for the cotton industry. Here, too, the Keiretsu were valuable in that they gave trading companies the flexibility to sell a range of products from staple and filament to cloth and apparel. When import restrictions began to threaten the industry's export position, they usually struck at the final stages of production—spinning, weaving, or apparel manufacturing. As export agents, the trading companies were generally the first to recognize such threats. Confronted with the need to establish local manufacturing facilities, both the fiber manufacturers and the trading companies saw the advantages of the Keiretsu. Neither had operating experience or skill in any of the downstream operations; nevertheless, they were able to provide the needed specialized skills by calling on Keiretsu manufacturers who would have been hesitant to go abroad by themselves but were willing to do so with the backing of a fiber manufacturer and a trading company. The local subsidiary then became a captive outlet for the export of intermediate materials from the Japanese fiber manufacturer through the agency of the trading company.

Between 1959 and 1973 the eight leading Japanese synthetic fiber manufacturers established 114 subsidiaries abroad in apparel manufacturing, spinning, dyeing, and weaving. All but four of them were joint ventures involving at least a fiber manufacturer, a trading company, and a downstream Keiretsu firm. A typical 20 to 30 percent of the equity was held by the fiber manufacturer; 15 to 25 percent by one trading company or sometimes a combination of several; and 5 to 10 percent by a Keiretsu firm. The remainder of the equity was usually held by local interests.

The Keiretsu offer a number of advantages. First, a Keiretsu gives a small Japanese subsidiary abroad performing only limited manufacturing operations benefits associated with vertical integration. Since it imports most of its intermediate materials from the larger enterprise with which it is associated, it gains from the economy of scale in production at the fiber stage. The local subsidiary can also obtain credit from the Keiretsu's trading company at favorable terms, not an insignificant competitive advantage, particularly in a developing country. Since its output is marketed locally through the trading company, it also benefits from the economy of scale in distribution. Moreover, it has direct access to new technological developments generated by the Keiretsu parent company in Japan. The intimate relationship nurtured through years of close association and the mutuality of interest sustained by closely interwoven interests in Japan facilitates communications among the various partners in the subsidiary.

The Keiretsu relationship was used in a similar manner by major steel manufacturers as they established small plants abroad to defend their export markets for their fabricated products. Indeed, Keiretsu provided a unique competitive advantage to Japanese firms in the industries with standard and mature products. Surely Du Pont, Celanese, and U.S. Steel were not in a position to enjoy the advantages associated with Keiretsu, a distinct product of the Japanese economic and social system.

Certain Japanese industries enjoyed yet another competitive advantage, deriving from the fact that the particular requirements of their domestic market were quite similar to those of developing countries. This was most notable in the consumer electronics and home appliance industries. For one thing, Japanese manufacturers had to accommodate their product designs to the small size of Japanese homes. Space-saving features were also important in most developing countries. Furthermore, the Japanese consumer electronic and appliance industries began in the mid-1950s by producing rather rudimentary products, such as electric fans and irons. The domestic demand for these products was quickly saturated and began to decline. In slightly more than a decade, Japanese consumers upgraded in their purchases moving first from irons, fans, and transistor radios to small refrigerators, washing machines, and standard black-and-white television sets; then to products associated with high-income markets—vacuum cleaners, air conditioning units, and electric ranges. At its height, however, the demand for basic products was large. Particularly after the products had attained maturity, major manufacturers competed intensely developing considerable sophistication in the engineering, production, and design of these rudimentary products. When they moved into developing countries, the experience was recent enough to be readily mobilized. Thus, the particular stimuli of the domestic market provided an advantage for certain Japanese industries when they moved abroad, just as they had, though in a very different way for certain U.S.-based multinational enterprises.

The Search for Stability

These advantages, however, were not enduring. By the mid 1960s, it was becoming increasingly apparent that whatever oligopolistic advantages had existed initially were in serious danger. The most fundamental source of this vulnerability, of course, lay in the very nature of the industries and operations in which Japanese enterprises had concentrated.

Activities like the manufacture of apparel and textiles, weaving, metal fabrication, and the assembly of rudimentary consumer electronics and home appliances were relatively easy to imitate, even for local entrepreneurs. Technologies were simple and well diffused, and scale requirements quite limited. And indeed, new firms entered these fields in considerable numbers. Consider the example of Thailand, the major staging area for Japanese investment in the 1960s. In about 1960 the Thai government began to pursue import substitution programs by offering various incentives and protections for firms in certain industries to undertake production within the country. The period between 1960 and 1967 saw the establishment of 23 new textile-spinning plants—of which 14 were Japanese joint ventures—and 27 textile-weaving plants with more than 100 employees—of which 16 were at least partially owned by Japanese interests. At the same time, more than a dozen manufacturers of consumer electronics and home appliances were established; 17 new plants were built in metal fabrication; and 8 firms entered into the assembly of automobiles and motorcycles. Such a proliferation of small highly fragmented operations led to the predictable consequences of overcapacity, keen price competition, and rapid decline in profit.

In textiles and metal fabrication, the Keiretsu advantage was not sufficient to hold down the number of competitors. Intermediate materials, such as synthetic fiber or sheet metal, were readily available from other sources. The costs of being a part of a large complex corporate system began to outweigh the economies. Furthermore, it began to become clear that there were certain diseconomies associated with the Keiretsu. Decision making, for example, tended to be slower partly because of the number of partners involved. Moreover, although the partners usually had strong common interests, they were still independent companies, each anxious to maintain its own representative in the management of a local subsidiary.

In consumer electronics and home appliances, rudimentary products manufactured in large quantities in Taiwan and Hong Kong began to enter other Southeast Asian markets through Chinese trading networks. Most of the Japanese subsidiaries lost their initial competitive advantage over local competitors.

To defend themselves in the local markets, Japanese enterprises adopted several strategies that were familiar elements in U.S. multinational enterprises in mature oligopolies. First, they upgraded and expanded their product lines. This strategy, particularly notable in consumer electronics and home appliances, is clearly illustrated by the changes in the product mix of 17 Japanese subsidiaries manufacturing consumer electronics in Taiwan, Thailand, and Malaysia. All 17 firms were established between 1962 and 1967—all but four initially producing lower-priced transistor radios. Of the remaining four firms, two began with batteries, and the other two skipped the transistor radio stage and began by assembling black-and-white television sets. Within three years after their establishment, all but two of the subsidiaries were assembling black-and-white television sets—a line which soon became their major one. Within five years, nine firms had begun to assemble color television sets. Similarly, the home appliance manufacturers started by producing irons and electric fans, but soon added refrigerators and then such items as vacuum cleaners and room air-conditioning units.

The second strategy employed extensively was product differentiation, through the active promotion of brand names. Japanese manufacturers of consumer electronics and home appliances, for example, had already built formidable entry barriers into their domestic market through product differentiation. As their products came under increasing competitive pressures overseas, they turned to the strategy which had worked well at home. For example, every one of the 17 consumer electronics subsidiaries just discussed reported a steady increase in the absolute volume of advertising expenditure and in the percentage of total sales devoted to advertising. Other indications of the growing emphasis on marketing in these firms includes a rapid increase in their budgets for strengthening dealer organizations and the fact that all but two of them had added marketing managers from Japan during the three year period ending in 1973.

A number of Japanse manufacturing firms also began to pursue a strategy of vertical integration. In the synthetic fiber industry, for example, the first to act were the two leaders, Toray and Teijin, in Thailand. By the mid-1960s both companies had established a half dozen small subsidiaries, performing various downstream operations, from spinning and dyeing to weaving and apparel manufacturing. As local firms and Japanese competitors began to elbow their way into the field, the firms' competitive advantages quickly eroded at these stages. Toray and Teijin sought to recapture their oligopolistic advantages by entering into fiber manufacturing. In the late 1960s Toray established a nylon plant, and Teijin began to manufacture polyester fiber. Fiber production, unlike other aspects of textile manufacturing, is a capital-intensive operation, where the economy of scale is an important factor. The barriers of entry at this stage are considerably greater than those at downstream stages.

Now that they were acutely aware of the competitive vulnerability of downstream operations, the two companies sought to pursue a strategy of vertical integration from the outset in subsequent entries into new major markets. When Toray entered Indonesia, for example, it built a nylon plant at the same time that it expanded into downstream operations. Subsequently, the company went a step further by entering into the production of capolactum, the primary raw material for the production of nylon. Teijin committed itself to a similar strategy of vertical integration in Indonesia by establishing a joint venture with Pertermina, Indonesia's national oil company, to produce D.M.T. and paraxylene, the two basic chemicals used in the production of polyester fiber. Entry barriers to the production of chemicals are even higher than they are to the production of fiber.

Still a fourth strategy employed by an increasing number of Japanese firms to recapture their competitive advantages was to seek system-wide benefits by building multinational networks. Initially, each subsidiary served a local market, maintaining no direct ties with other foreign units. As the local subsidiaries began to face keen competition, however, the Japanese parent companies became aware, as their U.S. counterparts had earlier, of the benefits to be derived from coordinating the production plans of the various subsidiaries and from the cross-hauling of products among them. Such cooperation would enable each subsidiary to benefit from the economy of scale and also to capitalize on the differences in factor costs in various countries.

In the early 1970s the strategy of forging close multinational links was just beginning, as is evident in the aforementioned MITI survey of 661 manufacturing subsidiaries. On the average, less than 19 percent of the total sales of the subsidiaries went to outside markets other than Japan, and less than 5 percent went back to Japan. There was considerable variation according to the industry. (See Table 3-7.)

A few internationally experienced companies, however, had made considerable progress toward building multinational links. Teijin's D.M.T. and paraxylene plants in Indonesia were to supply not only the local market but the company's other foreign affiliates as well, for the local market alone was not large enough to support the scale of production needed for efficient operation.

Toray, Teijin's major competitor, has been pursuing a multinational strategy of a different sort. In 1973 it entered an extensive agreement with the Hong Kong-based Textile Alliance Ltd. to strengthen the company's multinational network in downstream operations. TAL, a major integrated textile firm jointly owned by Jardine, Matheson of Great Britain and a local entrepreneur, had 30 mills with a total annual capacity of 16 million yards of cloth, as well as a large number of apparel manufacturing facilities in several Asian countries. TAL also had a strong sales network in Europe, the United States, and Asia which handled an estimated annual sales volume of over $100 million.

Toray, which had been a supplier of fibers to TAL since the early 1960s, acquired a 30 percent interest in the firm in 1972. Since then Toray began to supply many of TAL's requirements for intermediate materials from its plants in Japan as well as from those in foreign countries. Toray also established several joint ventures with TAL in various phases of textile manufacturing in Thailand, Hong Kong, Indonesia, Malaysia, and Singapore.

A number of manufacturers of consumer electronics and home appliances have also begun to pursue a strategy of building a multinational network. As an initial step, several Japanese manufacturers built plants in Korea, Taiwan, and Malaysia to manufacture parts and components for other subsidiaries and even for the parent companies in Japan.

Similarly, in the mid-1970s leading Japanese automobile manufacturers began to explore the feasibility of exporting from their foreign subsidiaries and building several major parts manufacturing centers in various parts of the world. For example, Nissan, a leading Japanese automobile manufacturer had begun to export trucks to several Latin American markets from its Mexican subsidiary, the largest Japanese automobile plant overseas. This export operation, though partially motivated by the Mexican government's requirements, was considered important to the subsidiary in competing effectively in the Mexican market where major U.S. and European automobile manufacturers had the advantages of a strong established position and ready access to other markets through their multinational links. Nissan has also begun to integrate production among several countries in Southeast Asia. It has established a plant in Malaysia to manufacture several standard components both for the local market and for the company's affiliates in Thailand, Singapore, and Indonesia.

Still a fifth defensive strategy by which Japanese enterprises had begun to seek stability involves entering into cooperative arrangements with other major Japanese or foreign competitors. The forces which triggered cooperative behavior in the oil industry began to make themselves felt in certain manufacturing industries as well. The propensity of U.S.-based multinational enterprises in mature oligopolies to form joint ventures and other kinds of cooperative arrangements has been noted.[10] Such arrangements allow the participants to observe each other's behavior including cost structure. It also builds a community of interest among the rivals, thereby increasing their propensity for cooperation. In the domestic market, firms are usually fairly familiar with the cost structure of their competitors and the interests of rivals are intricately interwoven. As the Japanese enterprises begin to operate in unfamiliar territories, however, any measures which help build mutual interests among their foreign manufacturing activities are especially valuable.

By the mid-1970s several cooperative arrangements had appeared among Japanese enterprises, Toray and Teijin sought each other's equity participation when they established nylon and polyester fiber plants in Thailand. Although both companies actively produced both fibers in Japan, the limited size of the market in Thailand made some sort of understanding necessary. Thus, they arranged that Toray would produce nylon, Teijin polyester, and that they would exchange minority shares in each other's ventures. After the two companies reached this understanding in Thailand, it was extended to other major markets, such as Brazil and Indonesia, where both companies were active.

Similarly, Toyota and Nissan, Japan's two leading automobile manufacturers, have agreed to build joint facilities to manufacture engines in Australia to supply their respective assembly operations. Not only will these common production facilities provide the two firms with the economy of scale, but they will also tend to bolster the stability of this market.

The strategy of seeking stability through cooperative arrangements began to include multinational enterprises of other national origins as well as those of Japanese origins. Foreign rivals pose an even more serious threat to Japanese multinational enterprises than their Japanese counterparts because they are unfamiliar with the operations of such companies, and lack the extensive interdependence in the domestic market so often found among Japanese rivals. Such cooperation across national lines is most notable in the automobile industry, which is taking on more and more signs of mature oligopoly.[11] Isuzu and General Motors, partners in operations in Japan, have jointly developed new models for the Japanese market as well as for export markets. They have also begun to collaborate in manufacturing activities in Southeast Asia. General Motors has agreed to assemble Isuzu's trucks in Malaysia, the Philippines, New Zealand, and Australia, Honda and Ford have also entered cooperative arrangements. In 1973 Honda signed an agreement to market Ford's automobiles in Japan, and subsequently the two companies decided to strengthen their ties through a collaborative relationship elsewhere. In 1974 they were exploring the possibility of having Ford manufacture and market Honda automobiles in the Philippines.

Defense of the Market Position in Advanced Countries

In the late 1960s, Japanese industries began to face a threat of another sort in major export markets—this time in advanced countries, particularly the United States. The importance of the United States as an export market for Japanese industries is underscored by the fact that ever since the mid-1950s the United States has consistently absorbed over a third of all Japanese export. Over 50 percent of the export from some industries goes to the United States. Until the late 1960s Japanese export had enjoyed strong competitive advantages in the U.S. market in a wide variety of industries, including textiles, steel, electronics, automobiles, and chemicals. Japanese productive capacities were increasing so rapidly that they consistently outpaced wage increases. In the late 1960s, however, the accelerating rate of maturity of many of Japan's exports and the rising wage level at home began to erode Japan's once formidable competitive advantages in a number of fields.

The consumer electronics industry serves as an excellent example. By the late 1950s a few standard products, particularly transistor radios and black-and-white television sets, had begun to manifest signs of maturity in the U.S. market. The price had become increasingly important as a competitive tool. American manufacturers of these products had become aware that the economy of scale alone was not sufficient to limit the number of competitors to the level needed to sustain an oligopolistic equilibrium. They sought to prolong the existing equilibrium by intensifying their investment for product differentiation through brand names. These efforts proved only partially successful. Much to their concern, the cross-elasticity had become uncomfortably high. The American manufacturers realized that the future of their industry was insecure and that their survival would depend on cost and price considerations. At first, U.S. manufacturers and mass merchandisers turned to the rapidly growing electronics industry in Japan to buy inexpensive parts, components, or even lower-priced lines of assembly products.

This American strategy was reflected in the rapid increase in Japanese export of standard electronic products to the United States beginning in the late 1950s. For example, the export of transistor radios to the United States tripled in one year between 1958 and 1959 and, during each of the subsequent three years, increased again by over 30 percent. Similarly the export of black-and-white television sets to the United States doubled between 1960 and 1961, then increased again by nearly seven times during the subsequent two years.[12]

With rapid increase in Japanese wage levels, however, Japan's advantage gradually eroded. Meanwhile, among these products, the maturing process was accelerating, and cost was becoming even more important. By this time, leading U.S. manufacturers of consumer electronics had become multinational and developed internal capabilities to scan costs throughout the world.

They could shift their procurement points from Japan to other countries without much trouble. Many of them already had manufacturing subsidiaries in some of the low-wage countries to serve local markets; by simply expanding the scale of these subsidiaries, they could use them to supply the U.S. market as well. In some cases, American firms merely set up purchasing organizations to seek out low-cost independent suppliers. In most instances, however, they established their own production facilities, a procedure that made it easier for them to maintain strict quality requirements and delivery schedules.[13]

Such moves by American firms posed a major threat to Japanese manufacturers of consumer electronics. Between 1965 and 1970, for example, the share of the U.S. import of black-and-white television sets that came from Japan declined from 95 to 28 percent, of transistor radios from 79 to 54 percent. The same thing happened in basic parts and in components used for standard consumer electronics products. The Japanese share of the U.S. import of condensers, for example, declined from 66 to 36 percent during the same period. At this point, the Japanese manufacturers could have stopped exporting the lower-priced lines and shifted their emphasis to higher-priced items and other products, but they were reluctant to do so, largely because the sales of the lower-priced products generated externalities important to the sale of other products. Moreover, the Japanese firms recognized that it was only a matter of time before even the higher-priced lines would become vulnerable to foreign competition. Thus, what Japan's leading electronics manufacturers did was to match the actions of American firms by establishing their own production facilities in low-wage countries to supply the U.S. market.

The factors that made American enterprises reluctant to depend on independent suppliers were even more compelling to Japanese than to American manufacturers. The fact that American buyers still felt a lingering uncertainty about the quality of the Japanese products made the assurance of quality extremely important in the sales of Japanese products. Moreover, since Japanese manufacturers sold their products to American manufacturers and mass merchandising firms, instead of through their own outlets, strict adherence to delivery schedules was a crucial competitive tool. Furthermore, since the Japanese firms sold products to a number of different customers in the United States, they had to make rather frequent adjustments concerning the products and models to be manufactured by their off-shore facilities. This created a need for frequent communication among the various elements within the corporate system, including the sales subsidiary in the United States, the export division, the product division, and various plants in Japan that produced similar items. Finally, by this time Japanese electronics manufacturers had developed a highly rationalized production system to meet the growing competition in both domestic and foreign markets, and they were anxious to transfer it to their suppliers, a process that would be much easier if they owned the plants than if the suppliers were independent.

These initial moves abroad by major Japanese companies were soon followed by manufacturers of electronic parts and components. Between 1951 and 1972 Japanese electronics manufacturers created 224 manufacturing subsidiaries abroad, a total investment of about $120 million. About 60 percent of these investments were made between 1965 and 1972, and an estimated half of the output, measured in terms of value, was exported abroad, primarily to the United States. Investment is heavily concentrated in Asia, particularly in Taiwan, Korea, and Hong Kong (see Table 3-8), the countries noted for the availability of abundant low-cost labor of excellent quality. Taiwan and Korea, moreover, are former colonies of Japan, so the Japanese tend to be familiar with conditions there.

Investment in the United States

Until the early 1970s, Japanese manufacturing investments were confined almost entirely to developing countries. What few investments there were in advanced countries seem to have been idiosyncratic in character. This was quite understandable. The entry barriers to advanced markets, particularly the United States, were formidable. Wages were much higher; management practices were unfamiliar. Most Japanese firms had acquired their technology and marketing skill from American enterprises—technology primarily through licensing and marketing skill largely through observation and imitation. Hence, save for a few exceptions, they lacked oligopolistic advantages of any sort over their American competitors in these areas. Furthermore, Japanese industries had no strong incentives for investing in the United States as long as they were able to serve the American market through export, an area where, through a combination of scale and lower wages, they had a competitive advantage.

By the early 1970s, however, rapidly narrowing wage levels coupled with two currency realignments had reduced the cost differential between the two countries. A study released by the Industrial Bank of Japan in the spring of 1974 reported that by 1975, because of the combined effect of rising wages, revaluations, and the increasing price of materials, the production costs of standard radios and television sets in Japan would probably exceed those in the United States.[14] United States import restrictions were also threatening Japanese export quite seriously. Despite these threats only a very few types of enterprise were able to surmount the barriers and enter the United States.

For firms in mature oligopolies, the most serious entry barrier was in the form of a scale. As a first condition, therefore, to investing in the United States, an enterprise had to have a substantial enough market position there to enable it to produce on a large scale. One industry that met this condition was the ball-bearing industry. With the help of a rapid increase in domestic demand and the severe restrictions against import imposed by the Japanese government, the Japanese ball-bearing industry had achieved tremendous growth during the 1950s and 1960s.[15] The four major firms, which together commanded 75 percent of the domestic market, competed vigorously to expand their capacities. By the mid-1960s the Japanese industry had the second largest capacity in the world and was the world's largest exporter. The tremendous increase in the quantity of Japanese ball bearings entering the United States posed a serious threat to the American manufacturers. By the mid-1960s the U.S. government had begun to impose import barriers and the U.S. Department of Defense placed its own even stricter restrictions on the procurement of foreign manufactured ball bearings for military use. In this industry, the assurance of delivery is a critical consideration, because disruption in supply is likely to cause extremely costly delays in an entire production process.

These forces led Japanese manufacturers to consider manufacturing within the United States. The leading firms had built a large market in the United States, sufficient to enable them to attain scale economy. Their entries were further facilitated by a highly efficient and automated production system which minimized, for Japanese manufacturers, the problems associated with having to deal with a large number of American workers. In 1971 Toyo Bearing established its first plant in the United States. By the end of 1973 three others had established manufacturing facilities.

Consumer electronics is another industry in which export scale and product differentiation have enabled a few firms to achieve successful entry into the United States. In the early 1970s Sony built a plant to manufacture color television sets in Southern California, becoming the first Japanese firm in this field to set up manufacturing facilities in the United States. In approaching the export market, Sony had chosen to sell its products under the company's own brand name in contrast to the usual Japanese approach of selling through the brand names of American manufacturing or mass merchandising firms. Moreover, in the United States, instead of concentrating on the lower-priced lines typical of other Japanese manufacturers, the company emphasized products with innovative concepts suited to high-income markets. These were radical strategies for Japanese companies in the late 1950s. It started exporting transistor radios in the 1950s and portable small-screen transistorized television sets in the early 1960s and color sets with some innovative features in the late 1960s. Using these products as a wedge and investing heavily in advertising, Sony became one of the few Japanese manufacturing firms to establish a strong brand name and marketing network in the United States market.

In the late 1960s, the company faced mounting pressures in the United States for import restrictions which were likely to threaten its ability to continue serving the U.S. market from Japan. The overriding importance to the company of the United States market—one which yielded a third of its total sales—led Sony to establish the plant in the United States. Not only was Sony able to meet the scale requirement, but it also enjoyed the oligopolistic advantages created through product differentiation, which helped overcome higher costs in the United States.

In the mid-1970s, several other investments have been made, based on similar competitive advantages of scale and trade name. Kawasaki Heavy Industries has built a major plant to manufacture motorcycles, and Nihon Gakki, Japan's leading manufacturer of musical instruments, has decided to manufacture its basic line of pianos in the United States.

In both ball bearings and consumer electronics, the initial move by one firm to establish a plant in the United States was quickly matched by other members of the oligopoly. In consumer electronics, Sony was followed by other major firms, namely, Hitachi and Mitsubishi Electric; in addition, Matsushita, Sony's major competitor, purchased the TV division of Motorola for a reported sum of $80 million. To a firm in either of these industries, the move by a rival firm to establish production facilities in the United States, the largest export market, presented a serious threat to equilibrium. The most obvious advantage to the rival, of course, was its ability to bypass import restrictions, but there were also more subtle ones including the acquisition of knowledge and experience which could be used in further expansion in the United States and possibly even in other advanced countries.

In the early 1970s, the dominant motives of a firm investing in the United States were to defend the export market and to counteract the actions of rivals, but a few sporadic investments have been sparked by other motives, particularly in high technology fields. By the late 1960s, as I have noted, Japanese enterprises had begun to encounter difficulty obtaining frontier technologies from foreign firms through licensing. To overcome this problem, a handful of firms have established small manufacturing subsidiaries in the United States with the objective of gaining access to professional engineering and research staffs conversant with a particular field of technology and, through them, to the American scientific community in related fields. Earlier similar motives had led a few European firms to invest in the United States, most notably Unilever, which gained valuable lessons in technology and marketing.[16]

Emergence of Large-scale Investment

In the early 1970s a new strategy was emerging in the multinationalization of Japanese manufacturing industries as the result of the convergence of several elements, as can be best illustrated by petrochemicals. The first element was a further change in the composition of Japanese export. Petrochemicals had become by the late 1960s one of Japan's key export items. The petrochemical industry in Japan began in 1960 when four groups —Mitsubishi, Mitsui, Sumitomo and Nippon Oil—almost simultaneously entered into the production of ethylene. The industry was one of the "target" industries of the 1960s and, with the active encouragement of MITI, it grew rapidly. The industry pursued a familiar strategy, absorbing the most advanced foreign technology and expanding capacity rapidly to gain the economy of scale so critical in this industry. Within less than ten years after its modest beginning, the industry had become the world's second largest producer of basic petrochemical products. The growth rate was particularly high between 1965 and 1970, when the production capacity for ethylene grew an average of 35 percent annually. By 1970 the industry had developed a temporary but quite serious overcapacity. As new facilities then under construction came on stream, the situation only worsened. In one year, 1972, three new 300,000 ton capacity ethylene plants opened, bringing Japan's total capacity to over five million tons. In view of this huge capacity and a glutted domestic market, Japanese producers began to intensify their export efforts. In 1970 alone the export of petrochemicals increased by 45 percent; in 1971 it increased again by 22 percent.

This increase in export was soon met by familiar import substitution programs in a number of major markets. In the early 1970s a number of developing countries, including Thailand and Korea, began to escalate their import substitution programs, restricting the import of familiar consumer products and semiprocessed materials and of more basic raw materials like petrochemicals. Countries with large oil and natural gas supplies, like Iran, Saudi Arabia, and Indonesia, had become especially eager to create petrochemical industries. Japanese manufacturers were faced with the necessity of undertaking local production in these countries to defend their markets. They were reluctant to do so, however, because of large investments required for production of basic petrochemicals and the small size of each local market.

Their initial hesitation, however, was overcome by a need of another sort, which by the early 1970s had become quite serious. By 1973 the outlook for domestic demand for basic petrochemicals had improved to a point where MITI and the industry agreed on the need to add two more 300,000 ton ethylene capacities by 1977. Once again, manufacturers began to engage in serious maneuvering for an advantageous position in the industry—vying for a slot in the MITI-sponsored program for the allocation of additional capacities. To execute another round of capacity expansion within Japan had become extremely difficult, however, because of the scarcity of plant sites. Because of stringent requirements for environmental control, the costs associated with building new plants there were increasing rapidly. There was also serious concern about the availability of raw materials. Thus, Japanese petrochemical manufacturers began to look abroad for sites to build incremental capabilities to supply the domestic market. This desire, coupled with the need to protect the export market, stimulated Japanese petrochemical companies to consider establishing production facilities abroad, particularly in those countries where petroleum resources were abundantly available.

The first project they undertook was in Thailand, where the Mitsui and Mitsubishi trading companies vied vigorously for local government licenses to participate in the manufacture of various petrochemical products. In 1973, after lengthy and turbulent negotiations, the final agreement was signed, calling for the participation of one Mitsubishi chemical firm with the Mitsubishi Trading Company and two Mitsui chemical companies and an independent petrochemical firm with the Mitsui Trading Company. All were expected to purchase naphtha from a local refinery to be constructed in 1976 jointly by Shell and Thai interests.

In 1974 another petrochemical complex was being planned in Iran. A group of Japanese firms, consisting of two Mitsui chemical firms and an independent petrochemical company under the leadership of Mitsui Trading Company, were participating in this complex in cooperation with the National Petrochemical Corporation, a wholly owned subsidiary of the Iranian Petroleum Corporation (I.P.C.). Unlike the Thai venture, in which Japanese interests were confined to downstream operations, the Japanese firms are to hold 50 percent of the ownership in the upstream operations here. The complex is also to include a 300,000 ton ethylene facility, for which the I.P.C. will supply natural gas as well as downstream operations.

Four companies closely related to the Industrial Bank of Japan announced a plan to establish a petrochemical complex in Canada as a joint venture with the Home Oil Company of Canada. In early 1974 the plan called for the project to obtain oil from tar to produce petrochemical derivatives. In addition to a refinery, it was to include an ethylene plant with a 300,000 ton capacity and facilities to produce low-density polyethylene, basic vinylon raw materials, and vinyl acetate. The output was to be marketed in Canada and exported to the United States and Japan. The Industrial Bank of Japan was playing the central coordinating role and was expected to seek equity participation for itself, and in a departure from the usual pattern no trading company was in evidence.

In mid-1974 several other major projects were under active consideration. Both the Mitsui and Mitsubishi groups were in the process of negotiating with the Korean government for participation in two major petrochemical complexes in Korea. A Mitsubishi group of companies was exploring the possibility of constructing a major complex in Saudi Arabia. Similarly, different Japanese groups, represented by different trading companies, were actively seeking entry into a newly planned petrochemical center in northeast Brazil. Opportunities in Singapore and Indonesia were also under intensive exploration.

What advantages can the Japanese petrochemical industry bring to bear on its foreign ventures? The products to be manufactured abroad are already in a mature stage. Some, in fact, are practically commodities. Save for a few very limited improvements in process, the technologies employed by the Japanese petrochemical industry are standard ones.[17] Thus the competitive advantages of Japanese petrochemical ventures abroad lie in a combination of scale and the unique Japanese system-based oligopoly.

Economy of scale is made possible by the fact that foreign subsidiaries were created to serve not only the limited local market but the Japanese market as well. The total ethylene consumption in Japan is expected to reach about 700 million tons by 1985—200 million tons more than the domestic production capacity of the mid-1970s. No doubt, a limited expansion of domestic facilities is feasible, but it will be impossible to meet all of the projected increase in demand through expansion in domestic capacities.

The other competitive advantage lies in the ability of Japanese firms to mobilize the uniquely Japanese Zaibatsu or bank-centered groups and trading companies to gain the advantages of a system-based oligopoly. Almost all the Japanese petrochemical projects are joint ventures participated in by related petrochemical firms and trading companies belonging to the same Zaibatsu or banking group. In putting together most large petrochemical ventures, the trading company which had acted as export agent for the petrochemical manufacturers has assumed a vital organizational role. This arrangement provides several unique advantages. First, the cooperative approach enables the participating firms to share the risks associated with a large-scale project. Second, the group's banks are quite willing to support joint projects sponsored by several firms within their group, so the venture has ready access to financial resources and is thereby able to overcome a critical entry barrier in petrochemicals—the large capital requirement. Third, such an arrangement can be an important asset in negotiating with the host government, since it puts the Japanese in a position to offer an integrated package, from ethylene production to downstream operations. Fourth, the presence of a trading company at the core gives the Japanese petrochemical ventures several distinct advantages. The trading company brings critical skills for negotiating and organizing large-scale ventures abroad, skills not possessed by petrochemical manufacturers. Also, the multinational network of the trading company helps provide the ventures with export opportunities, thereby enabling them to enjoy further economies of scale. Basic petrochemical products are well suited to distribution through trading companies. Finally, the trading company can assist in developing the market for petrochemical products locally by assisting its Keiretsu downstream processors and fabricators to establish plants within the country.

The examples noted indicate that the strategy of competitive matching is also evident here as in other industries. All the groups that were active in petrochemical manufacturing —Mitsui, Mitshibishi, Sumitomo, and Nippon Oil—matched each other's actions either in the same market or by entering other markets where roughly the same, if not more, advantageous conditions were found. Japan's leading petrochemical firms and trading companies readily saw the advantages that would accrue to rivals with production capacities outside of Japan. These advantages cover not only a foothold in an export market, but even more important, the capacity to serve the Japanese market from the foreign plant. For one thing, they would not be subject to MITI's control. Then, too, by entering into joint ventures with national oil companies in oil-exporting countries, they would enjoy secure access to raw materials. There always existed the possibilities that production costs would be lower in these countries than in Japan because of this favored access to raw materials and that the investment required for the plant with a comparable capacity abroad would likely be less abroad than in Japan. The risks of not matching competitors' moves loomed large in the minds of Japan's major petrochemical manufacturers.

Prospects for the Future

The initial oligopolistic advantages of small investments made in the defense of the export market quickly eroded. These investments were heavily concentrated in activity where entry

barriers were low. Faced with the loss of these initial oligopolistic advantages, Japanese enterprises began to adopt strategies
designed to prolong or recapture them.

How effective have these strategies been in arresting the decaying process? Because of their very recent origin, only frag-
mentary data were available in the mid-70s, but they tended to
suggest that fundamentally they did not enable firms in mature
oligopolies to maintain enduring advantages.

The strategies of expanding product lines and upgrading the
quality of products have not proven terribly effective because of
the limited size of the internal market in most of the countries
where the Japanese have made manufacturing investments. As
product lines expanded and models proliferated, production became hopelessly fragmented—a situation that resulted in high
unit costs. Japanese manufacturers soon found that the market
for expensive models and the products associated with high in-
comes was extremely limited. This problem was most acute for
the manufacturers of consumer durables, particularly consumer
electronics and home appliances.

Likewise, the strategy of product differentiation had inherent
limitations in developing countries where the size of the market
was small, discretionary income low, and means for implementing sophisticated marketing programs limited.

Often the strategy of seeking system-wide benefits through
multinational links also failed to realize its full potential for a variety of reasons, including the desire of local governments for
self-sufficiency, import restrictions, and the reluctance of local
partners to see the joint venture integrated into the multinational system of the Japanese parent firm. Moreover, because of
the very limited size of individual subsidiaries, many of the cost
advantages of a multinationally coordinated logistic system
tended to be offset by the cost of administering it.

The Japanese have had rather limited experience in seeking
stability through cooperative arrangements, but if the American
experience is any guide, they will find that such arrangements
do not always give enduring protection either. The strategy of
vertical integration as implemented in the synthetic fiber industry provides somewhat more enduring oligopolistic advantages. Entry barriers into fiber production are considerably
higher than those at the weaving or spinning stages. Nevertheless, the technologies involved are well diffused, and the scale
requirements are not prohibitively high as they are in some industries, so fiber production is within the realm of possibility of

local entrepreneurs. No doubt, small import substitution type investments will continue to appear but there are inherent limitations to their growth.

The search for lower-cost production facilities for standard products is almost certain to intensify as costs and prices take on increasing importance in so-called senescent oligopolies like consumer electronics where scale and product differentiation are of diminishing importance as barriers to entry. Japanese manufacturers of these products with an important stake in the U.S. market will anxiously seek to match the moves of large U.S. producers, and, if possible, gain temporary cost advantages over them. Japanese enterprises will be aided in these efforts by their growing capacity to scan the factor costs in different countries as they become multinational enterprises themselves.

Manufacturing investments in the United States are likely to expand from ball bearings, consumer electronics, and motorcycles to other fields. The most powerful galvanizing force here is the threat of import restrictions. An increasing number of firms will be in a position to command sufficient economy of scale to enter the United States and their chances of doing so will be enhanced by improved processing or product differentiation. Leading manufacturers of automobiles are very likely to invest in the United States in the near future. In 1972 the U.S. market accounted for nearly 43 percent of Japanese automobile export, as compared to less than 18 percent in 1965. During the seven-year period, the number of units exported to the United States increased from 34,000 to 8,400,000. In case they are confronted with a serious threat to the import of foreign automobiles, the two leading firms at least have built a sufficient market position to make limited production economically feasible.

The most enduring types of Japanese ventures abroad are likely to be those in which the economy of scale is extremely important—the petrochemicals ventures, for example, and those created, in part, to serve the large Japanese market. Access to the large domestic market would provide these investments with enormous scale advantages. Also, such investments are protected by Japan's unique system-based oligopoly in the form of a group approach.[18]

No doubt, Japanese manufacturing investments will grow, but their growth is likely to be limited by a fundamental weakness of Japanese industries—a lack, that is, of capacity to develop new technologies which would give them a commanding competitive advantage. Heavily concentrated in mature industries, Japanese manufacturing investments constantly face threats to their staying power and will experience a steady, sometimes quite rapid, erosion of their competitive advantages. Scale, trade names, and the Keiretsu—these things cannot provide lasting advantages, and the various defensive measures the Japanese have resorted to can only give temporary relief.

Since the mid-1960s Japanese industries have intensified their research and development efforts. Thus far, however, these efforts have led to few major technological breakthroughs. There is a general consensus in Japan among government officials, academicians, and the private citizens responsible for guiding Japan's research and development programs that, in the foreseeable future, Japan's capacity to generate highly innovative technologies will be quite limited except perhaps in certain specialized areas like environmental control where Japan is spurred on by her particularly strong needs.

A number of reasons may be cited for Japan's inability. For one thing, the nation lacks a strong rational scientific tradition, stressing originality and innovation.[19] Even more formidable is the relative lack of experience and capacity of Japan's major enterprises for coming up with original inventions or discoveries and, more important, for translating innovative ideas into new products. Most Japanese enterprises have yet to gain the capacity to mobilize the huge financial resources and organizational skills necessary to undertake large-scale research and development programs or to commercialize what innovative ideas they do have. The post-invention development of major products requires not only large sums of money but a long lead time.[20]

To compound the difficulty for Japanese enterprises, there is convincing evidence that, for the past decade or two, the economies of scale have become more and more important in the development of major new products, and this trend is likely to accelerate. To be sure many different kinds of process improvements will be generated by Japanese industries, but the advantages of material or cost savings process improvements are not very enduring. Japan's inability to generate major innovative technologies will almost certainly limit the multinational spread of her industries and will particularly inhibit any large-scale entry of Japanese manufacturing activities into the U.S. market. For the foreseeable future, then, Japanese enterprises will scarcely challenge the dominance of U.S.-based multinational enterprises.

Table 3-1. Number of subsidiaries created by the 43 Japanese manufacturing enterprises listed among "Fortune's" 200 non-U.S. enterprises, by year of establishment, 1957–70

YEAR	NUMBER	PERCENT
Pre-1957	74	20.0
1957–58	6	1.6
1959–60	15	4.1
1961–62	26	7.0
1963–64	41	11.1
1965–66	39	10.5
1966–68	68	18.4
1969–70	101	27.3
Total	370	100.0

Source: Harvard Mulitnational Enterprise study.

Table 3-2. Geographical spread of manufacturing subsidiaries owned by "Fortune's" 43 Japanese enterprises, 1951–70

LOCATION	NUMBER	PERCENT [a]
Asia	229	62.4
Latin America	62	16.8
Europe	18	4.9
White Commonwealth Countries	18	4.9
United States and Canada	17	4.6
Africa	17	4.6
Other	6	1.6
Total	367	100.0

Source: Harvard Multinational Enterprise Study.
[a] Because of rounding the total is not 100.

Table 3-3. Number of subsidiaries of "Fortune's" 43 Japanese manufacturing firms, by major product lines, 1970

PRODUCT	NUMBER	PERCENT [a]
Textiles	68	27.3
Electrical machinery	61	24.5
Transportation	25	10.0
Metal fabrication	25	10.0
Primary metals	19	7.6
Chemicals	13	5.2
Machines	16	6.4
Apparel	9	3.6
Rubber	5	2.0
Food	5	2.0
Instruments	1	0.4
Stones	1	0.4
Miscellaneous	1	0.4
Total	249	100.0

Source: Harvard Multinational Enterprise Study.
[a] Because of rounding the total is not 100.

Table 3-4. Number of firms in selected industries which established manufacturing subsidiaries within three years after an initial move by a competitor in three key markets, 1973

INDUSTRY	LEADING FIRMS IN A GIVEN INDUSTRY	COMPANIES WITH MANUFACTURING SUBSIDIARIES		
		TAIWAN	THAILAND	INDONESIA
Textiles	8			
Apparel manufacturing		8	7	7
Weaving		7	5	4
Spinning		6	5	3
Steel	5			
Galvanized ironsheet		2	5	5
Steel pipes		3	4	4
Consumer electronics and home appliances	7	7	6	4

Table 3-5. Average size of manufacturing investments in selected industries in Asia, by size of initial capitalization, 1973

INDUSTRY	AVERAGE SIZE OF CAPITALIZATION IN U.S. DOLLARS
Textiles	1,144,000
Nonelectrical machinery	805,000
Chemicals	419,000
Metals	220,000
Electrical machinery	127,000

Source: *Keizai kyoryokuno genjo to mondaitu*
(The current status and prospects of economic
cooperation; Tokyo: Ministry of International Trade
and Industry, 1974), pp. 632–633.

Table 3-6. Size of foreign subsidiaries owned by "Fortune's" 43 Japanese manufacturing enterprises, by sales, 1970

ANNUAL SALES ($ MILLION)	NUMBER OF SUBSIDIARIES	PERCENT OF TOTAL COMPANIES IN SAMPLE [a]
Less than $1	51	22.9
More than $1 but less than $10	136	61.3
More than $10 but less than $25	25	11.3
More than $25 but less than $100	7	3.2
More than $100	3	1.6
Total	222	100.3

Source: Harvard Multinational Enterprise Study.
[a] Because of rounding the total is not 100.

Table 3-7. Destination of sales of 661 foreign subsidiaries of 399 Japanese manufacturing enterprises, by industry, for fiscal year ending March 31, 1973.

INDUSTRY	LOCAL MARKET	OUTSIDE MARKETS OTHER THAN JAPAN	JAPANESE MARKET [a]
Metals	94.3	4.5	1.2
Transportation	91.6	8.9	0.5
Chemicals	89.1	7.3	3.6
Precision instruments	78.4	20.5	1.1
Textiles	75.1	22.4	2.5
Nonelectrical machinery	74.5	24.9	0.5
Electrical machinery	70.0	25.0	4.9
Sundry goods	67.4	23.8	8.8
Paper	18.4	42.1	39.5

Source: Showa 47 nendo wagakuni Kigyo no kaigai jigyo katsudo (A survey on
foreign activities of Japanese enterprises, fiscal year, 1972; Tokyo: The Ministry
of International Trade and Industry, 1973), p. 27.
[a] Because of rounding the total is not 100.

Table 3-8. Multinational spread of Japanese manufacturing subsidiaries
in the electronics industry, 1951–73

AREA	FINISHED PRODUCT ASSEMBLY	MANUFACTURING PARTS AND COMPONENTS
Total in Asia	71	98
Korea	16	26
Taiwan	17	55
Hong Kong	3	3
Singapore	6	7
Thailand	4	1
Malaysia	7	3
Other countries	18	3
Total in Latin America	23	6
Brazil	8	3
Mexico	4	1
Other countries	11	8
Other regions	18	8
Total	112	112

4. The Trading Company

Leading trading companies in Japan are often proclaimed as the forerunners of Japanese multinational enterprises. They have been the chief instruments of Japanese foreign trade for the past century. Few other enterprises in the world can match them for geographic coverage, diversity of product lines, and resources. Indeed, they have played a major role in Japanese ventures abroad in raw materials as well as in manufacturing.

Will the major Japanese trading companies, then, emerge as a distinct form of multinational enterprise? My research provides fairly convincing evidence that such transformation will prove to be most difficult. Though the trading companies have played and will continue to play important and varied roles in the multinationalization of Japanese industries, the prospects of these companies themselves becoming multinational enterprises with strong central system-wide coordination are limited indeed. My findings suggest that their primary role is likely to be confined to facilitating multinational moves by others. At first glance, this may seem a rather radical assessment in the mid 1970s, considering that all four Japanese enterprises most heavily involved in foreign direct investment in 1973 were trading companies. Closer examination, however, reveals that those very elements which had made trading companies such a uniquely successful global commercial organization would likely inhibit their ability to adopt strategies and structures necessary for transformation into multinational enterprises.

Strategy Toward Foreign Direct Investment

In 1973 the ten leading trading companies owned at least a 5 percent equity interest in 696 foreign affiliates. As in the area of foreign trade, the four largest trading companies—Mitsubishi,

Mitsui, Marubeni, and C. Itoh—led the way. Together they owned 496 or roughly 71 percent of all the subsidiaries owned by the ten largest trading companies. Although there were subsidiaries in every sector, over 65 percent of them were found in the manufacturing industries (see Table 4-1).

This active entry into manufacturing activities abroad may seem like a major change in the strategy of trading companies, which for decades have confined themselves almost exclusively to commercial activities. A detailed examination of the trading companies' investment behavior suggests, however, that their foreign manufacturing activities were merely an extension of their role as foreign trade agents. The force that triggered their move into foreign manufacturing was usually a threat to their export market. As the export agents for manufacturing enterprises, large and small, trading companies were generally the first firms to recognize any impending threat of import restrictions. In fact, their extensive facilities for political intelligence and their experiences in diverse product lines often enabled them to predict with fair accuracy the timing and form of such actions by foreign governments.

The trading company derived several important benefits from establishing a foreign manufacturing base jointly with a client manufacturing enterprise. Most important, it became the exclusive agent for supplying the new subsidiary with intermediate materials, components, and parts produced by the manufacturing partner in Japan. Because the subsidiaries were captive customers, the trading company was usually protected from the full rigor of competition and could exercise some flexibility in determining what prices to charge the subsidiaries. Moreover, the trading company could also benefit from the initial sale of equipment and machines to the local subsidiaries, since most could not be procured locally. In addition, forging a link with a large Japanese manufacturing company, even in the form of a minor joint venture in a small foreign market, had the potential long-term advantage for the trading company of creating a successful pattern for collaboration that might lead to similar ventures elsewhere.

Thus, like the manufacturers themselves, the trading companies usually made their initial moves into foreign manufacturing as ad hoc responses to specific threats. Typically, a threat was recognized in the context of day-to-day operations by those directly involved in exporting a particular product line. At this stage, the trading companies had no compelling incentive to engage in a systematic search for investment opportunities abroad. Their strategy was unambiguous, that is, to defend particular export markets and to become the major suppliers of intermediate materials or components, machinery, and equipment for the new plants overseas.

This strategy is reflected in the profiles of the manufacturing investments of trading companies. Subsidiaries abroad have been concentrated in industries for which the trading companies have traditionally served as export agents. Nearly 40 percent or 455 of them were manufacturing textiles or sundry goods, particularly cheap consumer goods. (See Table 4-2 for a classification of manufacturing subsidiaries by industry.) Of the affiliates classified under the metal, chemical, and machinery industries, the overwhelming majority were manufacturing or assembling standard end products. In the metal industry, investments were dominated by the production of galvanized iron sheets, steel pipes, and related products; in the chemical field, by the production of end-use plastic items, fertilizer, and so on; and in machinery, by the assembly of home appliances, automobiles, and farm equipment in marginal markets.

Most of the subsidiaries were quite small. Of the 413 manufacturing subsidiaries for which data were available, 268 (roughly 65 percent) were capitalized at ¥300 million or less; 166 (about 28 percent) at between ¥300 million and ¥3 billion. Only 29 were capitalized at ¥3 billion or more. Because exports began to encounter serious threats only in the mid-1960s, most of the manufacturing subsidiaries were also of recent origin. More than two thirds of them came into being after 1965, and more than one third between 1970 and 1973.

Since the trading company's major objective in undertaking foreign investment was to establish captive customers for their export, they usually demonstrated little desire to assume management control. In fact, they were anxious to limit their investment to a minimum—a strategy evidenced by the fact that, in almost all cases, the trading company's share in the joint ventures was quite limited. The ten leading companies owned 50 percent or more of the equity in less than 10 percent of their 455 manufacturing subsidiaries, whereas in nearly 68 percent of them, they owned 25 percent or less. (See Table 4-3.)

In the early 1960s, the trading companies began to become actively involved in raw material ventures abroad, as well as in small-scale manufacturing activities. The trading companies had been serving as import agents for iron, copper ores, bauxite, and other minerals. With the rapid increase in the consumption of these raw materials in Japan, sole reliance on straight purchasing arrangements became inadequate to assure an ever increasing supply. Spot purchases, of course, were most vulnerable, but even long-term contracts were not entirely satisfactory, since their terms were sometimes nullified by unilateral actions on the part of suppliers. Thus, to assure the necessary supply, trading companies, in cooperation with their major customers in Japan, sought to solidify their ties with selected foreign sources by extending long-term loans, in return for certain guaranteed supplies. In some cases, the trading companies strengthened their positions even more by buying a small share of equity in selected foreign mining projects.

In these minerals ventures, the trading companies sought to establish captive suppliers through whom they could supply the needs of major Japanese consumers; they used a similar approach to procure other resources, including pulp, timber, and food. In these cases also, they invested only to complement their chief function of importing, and, as was the case with their manufacturing investments, they demonstrated little interest, at least initially, in assuming management control in their raw material ventures.

Structural responses: the initial stage. The initial orientation of the trading companies toward their investment in foreign manufacturing ventures was characteristically short-ranged and rather haphazard, based primarily on their desire to maximize their short-run opportunities in trade to and from Japan. This outlook was understandable enough, since the trading company's main forte is to facilitate large-scale trading in standard products. Large trading companies are organized into divisions along major product lines, each of which has traditionally enjoyed considerable autonomy. In order to conduct negotiations and consummate deals throughout the world under various conditions, each division needs a detailed knowledge of essential products and markets and an ability to respond rapidly to changing conditions. In return for their autonomy, the product divisions are rigorously evaluated. With their transactions heavily concentrated in standard goods, they operate with a very low margin. Moreover, large trading companies have high fixed costs to support extensive global networks of personnel and offices. For these reasons, the trading company has traditionally placed a heavy emphasis on sales volume and rapid turnover of merchandise. Sales volume, traditionally the most important criterion for performance evaluation, is usually measured over a very short time span, scarcely longer than a semiannual accounting period. Such a control system further reinforced an organizational climate which placed a high premium on maximum exploitation of short-term gains.

Typically, a trading company's decision to become involved in a foreign raw material or manufacturing venture was made in an idiosyncratic manner. Since there was no central unit in the corporate organization to screen and evaluate such investments, managers in the product divisions had virtual autonomy to commit the company's funds to such a project in order to defend export markets or to bring about large sales of equipment or machinery. After all, the investments involved were typically small—seldom more than $200,000. Not infrequently, they were viewed as part of the cost of doing business, since they defended or generated export. A simple payback calculation based on the profit of the exports involved sufficed to meet the internal requirements of the trading company. In many cases, the potential penalties of not making the investment were impossible to calculate with any confidence. Thus, the product division was understandably inclined to take a defensive step, particularly when the investment required was rather small. Preoccupied with day-to-day commercial transactions, the product division staffs, however, had neither time, temperament, nor expertise to undertake thorough feasibility studies.

Unfortunately, once a venture got under way and the captive relationship was created, the product division seldom showed much interest in developing or nurturing the enterprise. Even the division's capacity to provide ongoing managerial or technical assistance to foreign affiliates was limited. This lack of continuing attention on the part of the trading company was particularly serious for ventures entered into for the sole purpose of consummating one-time sales of plant equipment and machinery, for once the sales were completed, the purpose of the investment was achieved as far as the trading company was concerned.

The common practice of sharing investment among several product divisions further diluted the interest of any one division in its foreign subsidiaries. Since each division was anxious to

limit its long-term financial commitments when a division became interested in a particular investment, it often sought the
participation of other divisions likely to benefit. An investment
in a textile weaving plant was typically made by the textile division, but the textile division might well entice the machinery
group to assume a share of the investment in return for the
exclusive right to sell textile equipment and machinery to the
new plant. In a number of instances, heavy arm-twisting tactics
were employed to force divisions that were likely to benefit from
a particular investment to contribute an appropriate share. Not
infrequently, in these circumstances, a reluctant division was
convinced partly by a tacit understanding that it might recoup its
investment by raising the price it charged the subsidiary for its
goods. Naturally, after the sale was consummated and the plant
got under way, the interest of these divisions in the subsidiary
generally declined rapidly.

By the early 1970s the major trading companies had entered
into a large number of small foreign ventures. Because of their
very extensive geographic coverage and the diversity of their
products, the trading companies encountered frequent threats
of import restrictions in different markets. For the reasons noted
earlier, competition among major trading companies was extremely keen, and all were anxious to maintain even their smallest markets. Typically, when confronted with a threat of import
restrictions in a given market, each trading company joined with
its chief manufacturing client to elbow its way into the market. It
was spurred on by the recognition that even in a small market,
its competitors would almost invariably take action against the
same threat.

By the early 1970s the product divisions had committed themselves to so many projects that in spite of the small size of each
one, they added up to an important financial commitment for
the trading company. Yet, by default, the trading company had
little influence over their operation. Even its small share of a
given subsidiary was sometimes divided among as many as four
or five autonomous divisions of the company, each with different interests. Neither the product divisions nor the headquarters staff exercised any formal control over the affiliates
beyond the day-to-day coordination of the flow of trade.

At this point, furthermore, many of the subsidiaries, which
had been ill conceived and quickly organized by the trading
companies to perpetrate export from Japan, were simply floun-

dering with no real hope of building stable operations. Because of their plight, they seldom attracted capable executives from the Japanese parent companies, and a vicious circle was established.

Noting the rapid increase in their financial commitment, trading companies began to be concerned over the plight of the faltering subsidiaries. Often their problems came to the attention of corporate headquarters in the form of requests for credit from the foreign subsidiaries. When the joint ventures were formed, the trading company often minimized its commitment of permanent capital by agreeing to provide liberal credit to the ventures for their purchase of intermediate materials from Japan. As performances faltered, however, the repayment of credits was often delayed and additional credit was requested. As the credit department, usually among the most powerful of the corporate staff groups, began to look into the operations of the subsidiaries, they became alarmed over the condition of a good many of them and at the careless manner in which they had been put together.

Faced with the poor performance of their foreign subsidiaries, the manufacturing firms, which tended to have greater shares of equity in them than the trading companies, were the first to become concerned. In many instances, they assumed the primary responsibility for improving the operations of the subsidiaries. They soon became disenchanted with the indifference of the trading companies toward the joint ventures and began to express their dissatisfaction to the trading companies' senior managers and corporate staff.

Moreover, the presence of small unprofitable manufacturing joint ventures often became a source of embarrassment to the management of the local branches of the trading company. In the small tightly knit business community typically found in developing countries, the news of poor performance by a local manufacturing venture spread quickly and created considerable adverse publicity. Repeatedly, the presence of a faltering subsidiary handicapped a local branch of a trading company in its dealings with local government and business interests.

Such pressures gradually converged until the senior managers and corporate staff of the major trading company recognized that the foreign investment behavior of the product divisions, if allowed to continue, could have serious long-term consequences. Although they still considered defense of the export market as a legitimate reason for the company to invest in manufacturing ventures abroad, they could no longer accept occupation with short-term benefits and lack of attention to long-term health of the new enterprise. Once a subsidiary was created, they realized, it took on a life of its own, one which continued to need care, feeding, and control.

To serve as the chief instrument for introducing a more coordinated or disciplined approach, a staff group specializing in foreign investment activities had been created in five of the six leading trading companies by the early 1970s. This marked the first formal structural response within the trading company to its strategy of investing in manufacturing operations and raw material ventures. In most companies, the group is called the Overseas Enterprise Department (OED) and is somewhat comparable to the international division in a manufacturing firm.

The road to legitimacy and acceptance for these OEDs has been a difficult one. The most formidable obstacle was the entrenched power enjoyed and jealously guarded by the product divisions. Initially, the product divisions saw little need for an OED. They felt that the life blood of the trading company was its commercial transactions—activities which, unlike those of manufacturing enterprises, did not lend themselves to systematic planning. They also argued that the most critical ingredient for the success of a trading company was the corporate and personal ties it had nourished during many years of satisfactory trade relationships.

The very diversity of the trading company's operations, in terms of both product lines and geographic coverage, further complicated the position of the OED, for it was unable to gain even a superficial familiarity with all of them. Thus, realistically, the OED could only offer planning expertise and try to provide supporting services for the product divisions in the form of evaluating and implementing new investments and helping the existing ones.

Some of the five Overseas Enterprise Departments have been more effective than others. In two companies where groups were established in 1971 and 1972, their impact was severely limited. The new groups in these firms were very small and tended to be overshadowed by the product divisions. Neither group was given full-fledged departmental status; one group was part of the planning and coordination staff, and the other was attached to an administrative services group which performed a variety of functions including liaison with overseas branches. The principal function of these two groups was to provide routine services relating to foreign investment; it had almost no voice in policy matters. Their involvement with new investments was pretty much limited to preparing an investment proposal after the critical decisions had been made. To this end they performed routine financial analyses, prepared pro forma statements, checked the credit standing of proposed local partners, submitted appropriate documents to the governments concerned, drafted joint venture contracts, and initiated, within the firm, the rather routine procedure for formal approval of the investment. The product divisions expected little from the newly created staff unit in the way of policy advice, and the group seldom challenged the premises of an investment.

There were reasons, however, why the creation of special staff groups had so little impact on these two companies. One of the two, a very large company was noted for its tradition of strong product divisions; it had always placed a high premium on independent entrepreneurial actions by product groups. The other firm, among the smallest of the six major trading companies, had made only limited foreign investments.

In the remaining three firms, with Overseas Enterprise Departments, the new groups at least partially met their original goals. After a period of groping for direction, the OEDs in these three companies had become increasingly realistic about their own capacities and limitations. They recognized that it was indeed appropriate that the primary responsibility for foreign investment rest with the product divisions. Only the divisions were in a position to identify new investment opportunities, to allocate funds to such investments, and to assume the risks associated with them. Gradually, the groups had begun to realize that the only way they could have impact on the product divisions was to build such a strong expertise at performing project analyses and feasibility studies that the product divisions could hardly afford to ignore their input. They also concluded that to be able to shape the character of particular investments at all, they had to assure themselves of opportunities to participate in the evaluation of potential investment projects at the earliest stage possible.

The progress achieved by the groups varied. In one company, for example, after painstaking effort, the OED persuaded the product divisions to agree to a procedure whereby proposals for new investments were to be prepared and submitted to top management jointly by the OED and the particular product division concerned. Even after formalizing this procedure, however, the OED experienced considerable difficulty for a while because it was called upon only in the final stages of planning to help draw up the formal proposal. As its competence increased, however, and it established stronger personal ties with the various product divisions, the divisions gradually accepted its desire to participate in the planning of new ventures in their early stages as well. To build its expertise, the OED engaged in active internal recruiting of personnel who had had some experience in project planning.

As its sophistication in planning and its analytical skills grew, the product divisions began to recognize its value. A well-analyzed and carefully drafted investment proposal they found was welcome not only by host governments but also by partner manufacturing enterprises, which often depended heavily on the trading company's analyses and projections in preparing their own proposals. Thus, the product divisions began to discover that the OED could be an important asset in dealing with potential partners.

In two of the firms, the OED managed to establish a committee to screen overseas investments. In one company, the Foreign Investment Review Committee, whose main task was to coordinate the activities of various overseas branches, consisted of the heads of several corporate staff departments, including Overseas Enterprise, Corporate Planning, Finance, Accounting, Credit Control, and Overseas Coordination. This committee evaluates each proposal and forwards its recommendations to the Executive Committee.

Prior to the creation of this group, each overseas investment had gone directly to the Executive Committee for approval—a procedure with several inherent weaknesses. The Executive Committee's agenda was usually so crowded that the amount of time available for each item was very limited. Moreover, except for two or three very senior members of the committee, each member had specific operating responsibility for one or more product groups—a responsibility which gave him a strong vested interest in certain proposals as well as a heavy work load. Altogether, the Executive Committee was not really able to give close and rigorous analysis to proposals for foreign investments which typically involved quite small sums of money. As a result, before the establishment of the new committee, such proposals had been routinely approved.

The creation of a specialized committee with the sole function of examining proposals for foreign investment went a long way toward correcting this situation. Significantly, the greatest benefit of this group derived not from its formal review of proposals per se but from the fact that its existence encouraged the product divisions to consult with the relevant staff groups ahead of time and to use the Overseas Enterprise Department as an intermediary in such consultations, thereby strengthening that group's position. The Japanese managerial climate characteristically emphasizes consensus; thus a particular group submitting a proposal is under enormous pressure to make certain that the proposal, once submitted, will be approved. This places a high premium on prior consultations to solicit the views of different groups and reconcile their differences. Now that approval was no longer routine, a final proposal was likely to be the result of considerable prior consultation, a process which tended to have a moderating impact even on the most assertive and dominant product divisions.

The establishment of such committees had also helped standardize the manner of data collection. In this company, for example, at the very earliest stage, when a project was still being explored by the principal parties—at the point when managers concerned thought there was at least a 50 percent probability that it would come to fruition—the OED encouraged the product division to submit a two-page initial proposal in a standard format, outlining the nature of the project, the required investment, the proposed percentage of ownership, the justification for investment, the division of management responsibilities among the proposed partners, and the potential benefits to the company. The project was then assigned to specific people in the OED who would follow up as it progressed. The initial proposal then served as the basis for a detailed feasibility study executed jointly by the OED and representatives of the product division. Not infrequently, at this point, representatives of the potential manufacturing partner joined the team.

While their effectiveness varied from company to company and even from project to project within the same company, the Overseas Enterprise Departments of the three companies paid particularly close attention to several major areas in screening new investment opportunities. First, they examined the objectives of an investment very carefully and attempted, not always successfully, to discourage investments justified solely by the opportunity they offered for export of intermediate materials over a short period of time or for one-time sales of equipment or machinery. They encouraged the product division to consider carefully and realistically the durability of the export market provided by the proposed subsidiary, relating convincing examples to show that minority ownership in a manufacturing joint venture would not always guarantee that it will remain a captive export outlet for an extended period of time.

Second, the OEDs made sure that the structure of an investment was sound and that the proposed enterprise had a reasonable chance of success in the local environment. They paid particular attention to the adequacy of the financial commitment. The OED tried to counteract the product division's desire to minimize the capital base of the subsidiary and to finance much of the operation through liberal extension of credit for the sales of intermediate materials from Japan, a procedure that minimized the exposure of long-term capital and made the subsidiary dependent on the trading company but left the subsidiary financially vulnerable as it increased local procurement of materials and decreased its purchases from Japan. To avoid these potential pitfalls, an OED encouraged an investing product division to provide adequate long-term capital to put a joint venture on a sound financial base from its inception. An OED frequently helped the sponsoring product division by negotiating with the corporate finance group for a lower interest rate or even an exemption of interest for a period of time. In addition, the OED also sought the participation of related product divisions which might benefit from the investment.

A third aspect of an investment that an OED carefully screened was the transfer prices of exported materials and the sales prices of machinery and equipment. The department checked the reasonableness of the prices charged by the product division. High transfer prices created serious tensions with local partners and often even with the local government and resulted in distrust and ill will which, once created, were very difficult to overcome. While continued monitoring of transfer prices was admittedly difficult, the OED's concern did seem to have a moderating impact on any design the product division may have had to exploit short-term gains.

A fourth common concern of the OEDs was the selection of

the representatives of the trading companies to be sent to the subsidiaries. While there was no established policy among any of the major trading companies, there was a rule of thumb that if a trading company's equity participation exceeded 20 percent, it would send at least one person to fill a key management position. Trading company personnel were quite reluctant to assume management positions in manufacturing subsidiaries. Despite a popular notion to the contrary, even an assignment to a well-established, major overseas branch was not necessarily attractive, particularly to those in the middle and upper management ranks. Unless the assignment was to one of a few highly coveted foreign posts, most personnel were anxious to remain at corporate headquarters, where important personal contacts might be maintained. Surely, assignment to small foreign joint ventures is considered less than satisfactory. Moreover, day-to-day management of a small foreign manufacturing joint venture would hardly present exciting challenges. Thus, in the past, two types of manager tended to be assigned to such ventures—managers who had approached or passed beyond the compulsory retirement age, who found in these ventures a last but often quite comfortable haven, and men who, though considerably younger, had rather limited career potential. Although, in the Japanese corporate culture, one could not formally decline an assignment once it was officially made, a person could use a variety of informal means to sabotage an assignment he considered highly undesirable. Moreover, senior managers in the product divisions were most reluctant to assign their more capable subordinates to distant affiliates. For these reasons, it was difficult for those responsible for planning a new venture to find a suitable executive willing to assume a responsible management position in the foreign affiliate. Thus, one of the critical tasks of the OED was to urge the product division to assign a well-qualified executive to the subsidiary. Of course, this arrangement had its own pitfalls: there had even been a few cases where an executive, annoyed with his assignment, aborted an investment through delaying or even sabotaging tactics.

A fifth major area in which an OED often attempted to influence a product division was in its choice of manufacturing partners for a joint venture. Whenever a choice existed, the OED urged the product division to give preference to manufacturing enterprises which belonged to the same Zaibatsu or banking group as a part of their overall effort to establish cohesiveness. Or they might suggest a particular manufacturing firm outside the traditional group with which the trading company wished to develop stronger ties. It became increasingly clear that the haphazard selection of manufacturing partners in the past had resulted in hopelessly tangled relationships in which a trading company found itself involved in joint ventures with several competing Japanese manufacturing enterprises in the same industry. This weakened the trading company's leverage in joint ventures, particularly as manufacturing enterprises became aware of the advantages of building an integrated multinational system and began to see the trading company, with its conflicting ties, as a hindrance. The OEDs argued that the systematic selection of manufacturing partners for joint ventures abroad might make it possible for the trading company to facilitate rather than hinder integration among various jointly owned affiliates, thereby joining the manufacturing partners in building a coordinated system.

Here again, however, the OEDs' success had been rather modest. The product divisions contended that, in practice, it was very difficult to select manufacturing partners systematically. The range of the choice was severely limited; a partner emerged in the course of exploration, and the relationship solidified only as planning proceeded. Moreover, the numerous personal relationships among the particular executives involved were critical in organizing a joint venture.

In addition to their efforts to influence new projects, the OEDs in the three companies had taken measures to strengthen their control over established subsidiaries. The proliferation of foreign ventures and the limited interest of most product divisions in the long-term welfare of their affiliates had led to an increasing awareness of the need to establish some sort of central reporting and control system to monitor the activities and performances of foreign affiliates. The original sponsoring product divisions had all but lost interest in an increasing number of affiliates, as export to them had declined or even ended altogether. Many of these subsidiaries have been struggling with little or no assistance from the parent trading company—a situation that had gradually eroded the company's influence in the joint venture.

The success of the OEDs in promoting the installations of reporting systems to keep abreast of the current status of foreign affiliates had varied. In the two firms where the OEDs were weak, no formal procedure had been installed as yet to serve as a liaison with joint ventures. One of the firms did have a small staff within a few product divisions which were particularly active in foreign manufacturing. The textile group, for example, had equity participation in 22 joint manufacturing ventures, of which 13 joint ventures with one manufacturing firm. This division had a middle management executive to serve as a liaison with these joint ventures, as well as with their parent companies. His functions, however, were confined chiefly to coordinating product flows and promoting close relationships with parent manufacturing companies in implementing new projects. In the second company, there was no formal control mechanism at all. The only time the condition of a subsidiary was ever examined in any systematic manner was when it sought additional lines of credit from the trading company.

In the remaining three companies, Overseas Enterprise Departments had been given formal responsibility for monitoring foreign subsidiaries. Their task was complicated by the number of subsidiaries, the diversity of their operations, and the varying degrees of ownership. A common approach followed by these firms was to establish crude priority classifications among the subsidiaries according to their relative importance.

In one of the companies, for example, the subsidiaries were divided into three categories. The first category consisted of joint ventures in which the company's ownership was less than 25 percent and in which, typically, it did not have a representative on the subsidiary's staff. In early 1973 nearly half of a total of 125 affiliates were in this category. Though it might have nominal representation on the board of directors, the trading company had little influence over these affiliates and received only semiannual financial statements and the minutes of the meetings of the board of directors. The OED was fully aware of the practical difficulty of trying to follow the conditions of these subsidiaries at all closely.

The second category consisted of affiliates in which the trading company had 25 percent or more ownership but less than a majority equity position and to whom the company had assigned a management representative. The company had 45 affiliates in this category, from whom the OED received brief monthly reports including financial statements. The presence of its own representative facilitates the trading company's communications with this group of subsidiaries. The OED routinely evaluated these reports and, whenever appropriate, identified problem areas and communicated them to the company's representative so that he could take corrective action.

The last category included those subsidiaries—four in all—in which the trading company owned a majority share of the equity. In each of these subsidiaries, several managers assigned by the trading company occupied key positions. These affiliates submitted detailed monthly reports to the OED. On each affiliate in these latter two categories the OED submitted a monthly summary report to the board of directors and the OED's manager made a brief semiannual oral report to the Executive Committee.

Despite the fact that this company had the most effective reporting system of any company I studied, its control was still limited, except, of course, where it had majority ownership. The OED staff consisted of only four individuals, and its manager was personally responsible for over thirty subsidiaries. With a total of more than a hundred subsidiaries to monitor, the group was constantly confronted with crises of some sort, and the special problems faced by a handful of subsidiaries absorbed most of their attention. They also had to coordinate expansion programs, approve additions of new products, and resolve conflicts between partners. Their task was further complicated by the fact that, since most of the representatives assigned to the subsidiaries came from the product divisions and hoped eventually to return to them, they tended to maintain direct ties to their divisions rather than to the OED.

Growing Threats

By the early 1970s, it was becoming increasingly clear to Japan's leading trading companies that their initial strategy of establishing small joint ventures in defense of the export market was threatened by a number of forces. The initial advantages associated with such ventures eroded quickly, and to recapture their competitive advantages they began to pursue new strategies, including adding new products, stressing product differentiation, seeking vertical integration, entering into cooperative arrangements with rivals, and seeking system-wide benefits through building an integrated logistical program.

As the subsidiaries began to pursue these strategies, the influence of trading companies typically declined further, since the manufacturing enterprises controlled most of the skills and resources necessary to implement them, including knowledge of the products, manufacturing technologies, and marketing know-how. Even in the area of finance, where presumably the trading companies had ample resources, they were often reluctant to help foreign subsidiaries expand, particularly when expansion would increase the subsidiary's self-sufficiency and decrease its dependence on export from Japan.

The manufacturing companies found at times that the presence of the trading companies as partners in joint ventures actually inhibited their efforts to pursue new strategies. This was especially true when they tried to build a multinational logistical system. Often, the various joint ventures of one manufacturing firm were often in partnership with a number of different trading companies, each of which was competing vigorously for a greater share of the intersubsidiary transactions—a situation which placed the manufacturing firm in the uncomfortable and difficult position of having to work out some sort of scheme for allocating business to the various trading companies.

The second powerful force threatening the initial strategy of the trading companies was the acquisition of experience in international business by a growing number of Japanese manufacturing enterprises. At the initial stage, manufacturing firms found the entry barriers external to Japan quite formidable. Typically, they had no experience in dealing with foreign governments, no appropriate local contacts, and a lack of staff which could do business in foreign languages. As they began to gain experience in foreign manufacturing, however, they found that the trading companies' knowledge of local environments was often disappointing. The central activity of the trading company—large-scale trading in standardized products—did not require any real understanding of the customs of their host countries. In distributing products locally, a trading company seldom went beyond primary wholesalers. As the manufacturing enterprises became seriously involved in foreign manufacturing activities, they soon developed deeper knowledge, greater expertise, and better local contacts than their trading company partners. The resulting conflicts were evident in a survey I conducted in 1972 among the 50 Japanese manufacturing enterprises with the largest foreign investments using trading companies regularly in their joint ventures abroad. I tried to identify what these manufacturing enterprises considered the major contributions of the trading companies as partners in foreign joint ventures and how they assessed the areas of conflicts they experienced with the trading companies.

My primary object was to determine why a manager responded differently according to the stage of international development his firm had reached. Specifically, I wanted to determine whether, as manufacturing firms gained greater experience in international business activities, they felt that the trading company's value to them declined. I divided the 50 firms into three groups according to the number of joint ventures they were engaged in. I considered firms with four joint ventures or fewer in an early stage of development; those with five to nine joint ventures in a moderately active stage; and those with 10 or more in an active stage. There were 16 firms in the first stage, 21 in the second, and 13 in the third. To adjust for different interpretations of the scales by different firms, I related a firm's scoring of each factor to its average rating on all factors. These normalized values facilitate a comparison of responses by the three groups of firms. (The results are presented in Tables 4-4 and 4-5.)

Some clear differences were notable among companies in different stages of international growth. In the early stage, the relationship between the manufacturing enterprise and the trading company seemed quite harmonious. Frequently, the trading company had initiated the joint venture by drawing the attention of the manufacturing firm to the investment opportunity. It also performed many useful functions for the inexperienced manufacturing partner, including investigating the investment climate, identifying an appropriate partner, and negotiating with the host government. This heavy dependence on the trading company was summed up succinctly by an executive of a major manufacturing enterprise in a personal interview. "When we go abroad, we are mute, deaf, and blind. We cannot speak the language, do not know the local customs and desperately lack useful local contacts. We need the guidance of a trading company." At this stage, the manufacturing firm also depended heavily on the trading company for staffing key management positions in joint ventures. The trading company's participation was reassuring to the managers of the manufacturing enterprises because it implied that the investment was sound and because they felt that it meant they could tap the resources of the trading company. In the eyes of an inexperienced manufacturing enterprise, the trading company enjoyed a great aura of international expertise.

In the moderately active stage, the manufacturing company's

relationship with the trading company remained virtually unaltered from the first stage. Since the internal competence and resources of the manufacturing firm was still quite limited, it continued to value the contributions of the trading company, especially its general knowledge and political connections. The managers of manufacturing companies in this group rated the financial resources the trading company could bring to bear more highly than did managers in either of the other groups. This is mainly because, although the firms at this stage had begun to commit themselves to the active expansion of their international activities, those in charge of international business had not yet attained sufficient stature within the organization to be able to tap corporate financial resources.

In the third stage, the relative value assigned by the manufacturing companies to their partnerships with trading companies declined drastically. The managers' rating in three areas—general management, marketing, and governmental relations—showed especially marked declines. By the time a manufacturing firm had reached the "active" stage, it had undertaken a number of major investments requiring most careful evaluation and planning. From their considerable operating experience abroad, they had accumulated substantial internal competence. For the experienced managers of these firms, the aura of great international expertise which once surrounded the trading company had all but disappeared.

Not only did the firms in the third stage attach less importance to the contributions of trading companies, they also assigned higher ratings to several major areas of conflict—sources of supply, transfer price, dispositions of earnings, and selection of expatriate executives.

The fact that by the early 1970s trading companies were gradually being elbowed out of large-scale ventures is clearly illustrated in the synthetic fiber industry. As fiber manufacturers, Toray and Teijin, began to pursue a strategy of vertical integration in the major markets, which included building large chemical and fiber plants, they underwent a definite change in their ownership policy. Whenever politically feasible, those two firms began to seek majority ownership of fiber and chemical plants. For one thing, unlike downstream operations, fiber production demands considerable technical input from the parent company. Moreover, where they created local fiber production capacities they stopped importing fiber from Japan entirely. Also, by this time, Toray and Teijin had developed the internal capability to initiate and manage large foreign manufacturing projects.

Of the twelve fiber plants the two companies established outside Japan between 1968 and 1973, seven did not include the participation of any trading company. In the remaining five, the manufacturers invited the participation of certain trading companies which had established downstream operations with other Japanese textile manufacturers in the particular market. By offering the trading companies a small share of equity in the fiber plants, the manufacturers hoped to create captive customers for their output—a particularly attractive prospect because fiber production is a capital intensive operation in which maintaining high level of production is very important. In these cases, however, unlike earlier ones, the manufacturers selected the trading companies and set the terms for their participation.

Another evidence of the eroding position of trading companies vis-à-vis manufacturing firms is the fact that a few internationally experienced manufacturing firms began to look beyond trading companies to find partners for joint ventures. Toray, for example, decided to enter into extensive collaborative relationships with the Hong Kong–based Textile Alliance Ltd., and Teijin entered an agreement with Monticattini to establish joint fiber production facilities in several European countries.

Emergence of New Strategies and Structures

In order to counteract these threats, major trading companies have begun to pursue several new strategies—strategies which in the mid-1970s were just beginning to unfold. First, trading companies have begun to shift their emphasis from small-scale ventures to large-scale projects involving petroleum, petrochemicals, and aluminum refining. As opportunities for these types of investment ripen, trading companies are seeking a central role as organizers and coordinators. A trading company can bring a number of distinct skills and resources to these projects, including its close connection with a number of manufacturing firms and financial institutions, its capacity to organize and implement large-scale foreign projects, its ability to amass large capital through its ready access to international money markets and its multinational commercial networks. These abilities place the trading company in a unique position to achieve a system-based oligopoly in large-scale ventures. The last two chapters have dealt with the unique roles played by trading companies in organizing large-scale projects in two major areas—the exploration for petroleum and the manufacture of basic petrochemicals.

A second new strategy of the trading companies involves strengthening their own multinational commercial network, so that they are able to facilitate rather than hinder similar efforts by manufacturing firms. Despite their extensive international network of branches and offices, trading companies have concentrated almost exclusively in trade to and from Japan. Until recently, trading among their various foreign units had been extremely limited—a phenomenon left largely to chance. Major trading companies, however, have become increasingly aware of the potential advantage of linking their widely scattered branches and operations. In their experience with large-scale projects in petrochemicals, steel, petroleum refining, and even minerals, they have found that their success to an important degree depends on their ability to market output outside Japan. Since they already have well-established positions in major markets, trading companies are in a unique position to provide the joint ventures with access to external markets so that they can enjoy the economy of scale.

As a first step, leading trading companies began to link major centers of operations. By the early 1970s the strategy was beginning to show tangible results. Japan's "third-country trade"—that which does not involve Japan either as a supplier or a market—increased considerably. For Mitsubishi this trade doubled in volume between 1971 and 1973 when it accounted for over 7 percent of its total trade. C. Itoh did $1 billion worth of third-country trade during the fiscal year ending on March 31, 1974, and intended to double that in two years. In this company, as in others, traditional commodities dominated third-country trade in 1973; soybeans, maize, and sugar, for example, accounted for nearly 65 percent of C. Itoh's third-country trade, textiles for 20 percent, and products of the chemical and heavy industries for only 15 percent. The company, however, was anxious to increase the relative importance of the latter.

The trading company's third strategy was to take an initiative in achieving vertical integration in key industries on a global scale. We have already seen examples of how leading trading companies have begun to link upstream and downstream operations in the petroleum industry. Mitsui has also purchased a 50 percent interest in the aluminum division of American Metal Climax thereby gaining access to rich bauxite reserves in Australia and refining facilities in the United States and elsewhere. Some of the output of the smelting facilities in the United States will be sold to Mitsui-related aluminum-fabricating firms in Japan, in which the trading company owns partial equity. Mitsui markets the fabricated products. Thus, Mitsui Trading Company has achieved at least partial vertical integration in the aluminum industry. This acquisition represented an investment of $125 million, presenting a striking contrast to Mitsui's first manufacturing investment of $42,000 in a glass bottle plant in Ceylon in 1958.

Still a fourth strategy being actively pursued by leading trading companies involves strengthening and diversifying operations in key markets. Various branches and subsidiaries located in major countries have now grown so large that they are significant enterprises in their own right. For example, the sales of the U.S. trading subsidiaries of Mitsubishi and Mitsui exceed $3 billion. In the early 1970s trading companies began to encourage these subsidiaries to diversify their operations beyond large-scale trading in standard products. Although only limited progress has been made so far, the direction of the thrust is clear. In a closely related attempt, several leading companies are trying to strengthen their technical and marketing expertise in order to broaden the product mix they offer in their major markets, particularly the United States. Mitsubishi, Marubeni, and C. Itoh, for example, have established wholly-owned sales subsidiaries in the United States to market products under their own brands, a significant departure from the traditional practices of trading companies.

As the trading companies pursued the new strategies, they began to make several structural changes—changes which were still in a very early and rather experimental stage in the mid-1970s.

First, as a step toward achieving greater integration, both multinational and vertical, leading trading companies have made a limited attempt to restructure their traditional commodity-based organization into one emphasizing system-wide integration and coordination. For example, several leading trading companies have created integrated energy divisions. Previously, each energy-related product, like coal or petroleum, was handled by a rather autonomous commodity group, which in turn was subdivided according to even narrower product lines. Moreover, within each group, procurement and marketing were performed by two distinct groups. By creating an energy division they sought to achieve vertical integration from the development of sources to the marketing of finished products and to coordinate various energy products so that they serve the varied needs of major customer groups better.

The second structural change has been the strengthening of staff functions concerned with diversification and with development of new ventures on a global basis. In all six leading companies, corporate development groups have been established to help the product divisions find new areas of activity, usually involving projects that require large investments. These groups have a capacity for project analysis and planning which the product divisions usually lack. Indeed, the size and complexity of the new projects and the long time horizons usually required for planning them demanded such a central staff. Moreover, since many of the projects contemplated by trading companies cut across traditional product lines, the corporate development groups play a vital coordinating role for the project: providing the initial impetus, arbitrating conflicting interests, and mobilizing diverse interest groups. The corporate development group also helps the product division mobilize external resources by doing things like identifying potential partners, negotiating the terms of participation, organizing a new entity, and recruiting key executives.

A third group of structural changes has been designed to implement the strategy of building multinational networks to facilitate the cross-hauling of goods among various foreign units. Various regional headquarters have been created. In 1974 Mitsui established regional centers in three major areas—the American continents, Europe, and Oceania—and assigned very senior executives to head them. In the same year, Marubeni established a European regional headquarters to be located in Brussels to manage and coordinate six wholly-owned subsidiaries, three branches, and five offices in Europe, as well as one branch and twelve offices in Africa. Steps are also being taken to achieve greater decentralization in order to give more power to the branch offices and wholly-owned subsidiaries.

The changes in the character of foreign investment by trading companies—particularly those in the direction of large-scale investment—make the future of the OEDs increasingly problematic. The initiative for planning and implementing a large-scale foreign investment project in resource development or manufacturing rests almost entirely with the relevant product division. In organizing a new oil venture abroad, for example, the petroleum division assumes responsibility; in undertaking a major manufacturing investment in, say, the petrochemical field, the chemical division leads the way. It is the product division that has the technical and industrial expertise, the knowledge of the market, and most important, the close contacts with major customers and potential collaborators. Moreover, it is the product division which must make a large financial commitment to the project and which is most affected by its performance.

In implementing a particular project, the representatives of the product division assigned to the particular branch negotiate with the host government and with potential local partners. The close and well-established relationship between the product division at the parent company and their local representatives leaves very little room for participation by the OED staff. In most cases, given the complexity of the project and the gestation period usually required, a special task force is organized within the division to undertake a feasibility study and to perform necessary planning functions. In dealing with certain products, like chemicals, the domestic and international trade are so interwoven that the division operates on a global basis, and its staff, many of whom have had a variety of foreign assignments, possesses extensive geographical as well as technical expertise.

Prospects for the Future

Major trading companies have been trying to become multinational enterprises engaged in diverse activities. Will they be successful? Is the trading company likely to become a distinct form of multinational enterprise?

Contrary to popular belief in Japan, the available evidence indicates that the answer is not very reassuring to the trading company. The traditional strength of the trading company was the scale on which it could procure and distribute standard goods. As Japan's industrial structure shifted its emphasis from textiles and sundry goods, to capital intensive goods, such as steel, chemicals, petroleum, and petrochemicals, the goods handled by trading companies underwent corresponding changes. The products they handled, however, continued to be mature, standard products bordering on commodities.

Since the late 1950s, when Japan began to export products that required technical services and extensive marketing efforts, the relative importance of the trading company in Japanese export has been on the decline. The marketing of consumer electronics, automobiles, precision instruments, and sophisticated machineries requires skills beyond those possessed by the trading company, and the marginal attempts of major trading companies to distribute these products have been highly unsatisfactory. The trading companies, almost totally excluded from this very important element in Japanese export, have been concentrating on products where oligopolistic advantage lay solely on scale—a fact that fundamentally inhibits their development into multinational enterprises.

We have seen how rapidly the initial advantages of marginal investments in standard products erode; there are reasons to suspect that the trading company's strength as a system builder and organizer of major international projects in manufacturing and raw materials will not be enduring either. True, the trading company is in an excellent position to organize and mobilize the resources of different enterprises. Once a large-scale project is organized and functioning, however, the trading company may not be able to play the central coordinating role it often envisions for itself. Indeed, in small joint ventures the trading company's relative influence tended to wane as its manufacturing partner gained experience and expertise in international business, particularly when it became seriously committed to its foreign activities.

Most of the trading company's advantages—knowledge of the market, local contacts, and an information network—though they are invaluable at the planning stage, tend to decline in importance rapidly as operations get underway, mostly because the manufacturing enterprises quickly acquire these assets for themselves.

Potentially, the trading company has two somewhat more enduring assets which it can bring to bear on large-scale joint ventures. One is its multinational commercial network, which could give local ventures access to external markets. Even here, however, the trading companies face some potential difficulties. Consider the case of petrochemical investments. As a given trading company becomes heavily involved in petrochemical production abroad, it will likely experience difficulties providing all of them with continuing access to external markets. The various subsidiaries, each wishing to maximize its own export, are likely to come into conflict with each other. The process is further complicated by the fact that subsidiaries located in various parts of the world are likely to have different manufacturing companies as partners.

The trading company's financial ability has been considered its second important strength. This too, however, has begun to show signs of decline. For one thing, an increasing number of Japanese multinational enterprises have been searching out financial sources themselves, developing ties with foreign and even multinational financial institutions, thereby reducing their dependence on Japanese banks and trading companies. A few Japanese manufacturing companies now have considerable sophistication when it comes to tapping foreign financial sources.

The trading company's financial strength has also been eroded by the emergence of Japanese financial institutions onto the international scene. Until recently, preoccupied with the rapidly growing domestic market and severely restricted by the Japanese government, Japan's major financial institutions paid little attention to the international market. By the mid-1970s, however, the situation has changed drastically. Government restrictions have loosened, and major Japanese banks have been lured into international expansion. As of March 31, 1973, when this trend was only beginning, Japanese banks already had 75 branches, 68 representative offices, and 21 subsidiaries abroad. This international expansion has taken a variety of forms. Like Japanese securities firms and other financial institutions, Japan's major banks have established commercial and investment banks abroad—some of them joint ventures with local interests. Quite a few banks have formed multinational banking consortia with major U.S. and European banks.

Perhaps the most serious factor inhibiting the transformation of trading companies into multinational enterprises is their management itself and the entrenched organizational climate nurtured by trading. In terms of size, diversity, and complexity, trading companies are almost unparalleled already, and their recent emphasis on diversifying beyond trading on a worldwide basis is only adding to these qualities. The traditional organization of trading companies as it is designed for trading activities is clearly inadequate; indeed, some structural changes are gradually being implemented. It remains to be seen, however, whether trading companies are flexible enough to develop an organizational structure and management which can provide system-wide benefits to highly diversified business activities scattered throughout the world. By and large, those who have come up the traditional career path in trading companies lack general management experience. The cozy relationship that has existed in Japan between major banks and trading companies is showing signs of strain. As growth opportunities with major industrial clients begin to saturate, banks have become increasingly interested in establishing direct ties with small- to medium-sized businesses.

As long as trading companies remained primarily configurations of relatively independent product divisions engaged in large-scale trading of standard products, the need and opportunity for strong central leadership and coordination was limited. Successful trading requires individual initiative, expertise, resourcefulness, and above all, an ability to respond rapidly. These very characteristics—those which made the trading companies so successful in the first place—are what make central coordination and planning so difficult. Because of the permanent employment system, change in Japanese corporations must come from within and therefore requires considerable time as well as persistent effort and education. The simple act of creating a new structure does not automatically change the entrenched and well-established orientation of the people involved.

A recent series of incidents highlights the difficulties of establishing effective central control. In the early 1970s, during the period of easy credit, trading companies rushed to invest their excess cash in securities and land. The leading trading companies made such large profits that, in one or two cases, their capital gains from stock and land transactions surpassed their operating profits. The public was aroused against what it considered excessively speculative activities. It was particularly concerned because aggressive and large-scale speculative buying was believed to be contributing to a rapid increase in land prices. Later, in 1973, when the oil crisis caused a temporary shortage in a variety of products, major trading companies were accused of blatantly exploiting the situation by hoarding essential goods—behavior which, their critics claimed, significantly accelerated the tempo of inflation. A series of parliamentary hearings uncovered many improper activities, some of them illegal. The publicity surrounding these hearings fanned the already growing public sentiment against business as a whole. The fact that apparently even the largest trading companies engaged in these activities reveals their vulnerability. Whether or not these activities were condoned or even tacitly approved by senior management is a moot point; what is critical is that the climate within the trading companies encouraged such behavior. Many point to these incidents as proof that, popular rhetoric to the contrary, the trading company's entrenched bias toward exploiting short-term gains had not changed.

One important issue in management revolves around the efforts being made to open up greater career opportunities for non-Japanese managers in foreign affiliates. Despite their many years of successful operations abroad, the managers of the trading companies' foreign branches and subsidiaries have, in the past, maintained close links with headquarters in Japan, links deemed necessary, since traditionally much of the trade took place with Japan and demanded close daily communication between the headquarters and the branches. Thus, the management climate in overseas branches has characteristically remained Japanese. Of course, the scope and size of such operations required a large complement of local employees. In 1973 Mitsubishi, for example, had 792 Japanese employees assigned from headquarters to affiliates abroad and employed 2,538 locals; Mitsui had 988 Japanese and 2,133 local nationals. In both companies, almost one out of four overseas employees was still a Japanese national from the parent company. Moreover, key positions were dominated by Japanese, and aside from a few token advancements, local nationals were seldom promoted to management positions with any real power or influence. Local employees were typically relegated to supporting positions with a minimum of responsibility.

The trading companies will no doubt continue to play vital roles as Japan's foreign trade agents. Their investments in raw material and manufacturing ventures abroad will certainly grow. For the reasons noted, however, their investments will be primarily ones which complement trade, and their chief role will likely remain that of facilitating multinational moves by others. Because of their particular areas of expertise and their highly entrenched organizational climate, it is quite unlikely that Japan's major trading companies will evolve into multinational enterprises with strong central control over their affiliates and system-wide coordination. In areas where they have already invested, the trading companies will face constant threats to their stability.

Table 4-1. Major activities of subsidiaries of the 10 leading trading companies, March 31, 1973

ACTIVITY	NUMBER	PERCENT
Manufacturing	455	65.4
Sales (other than general trading)	85	12.2
Service	83	11.9
Extractive	36	5.2
Resource development (other than extractive)	37	5.3
Total	696	100.0

Source: Company records.

Table 4-2. Foreign subsidiaries of the 10 leading trading companies, by industry, March 31, 1973

INDUSTRY	NUMBER OF SUBSIDIARIES	PERCENT
Textiles and related products	144	31.6
Metal	83	18.2
Machinery	68	14.9
Chemicals and related products	53	11.6
Food	37	8.1
Sundry goods	34	7.5
Pulp and paper	12	2.6
Other	24	5.3
	455	100.0

Source: Company records.

Table 4-3. Ownership patterns of foreign subsidiaries of the 10 leading trading companies, March 31, 1973 [a]

| | ALL SUBSIDIARIES | | MANUFACTURING SUBSIDIARIES | |
EQUITY OWNED	NUMBER	PERCENT	NUMBER	PERCENT
Greater than 95 percent	38	5.5	7	1.5
Between 50 and 95 percent	36	5.2	23	5.1
50 percent	45	6.5	15	3.3
Between 26 and 50 percent	142	20.4	95	20.9
Between 5 and 25 percent	422	60.6	309	67.9
Unknown	13	1.8	6	1.3
	696	100.0	455	100.0

Source: Company records.
[a] Excluding those established for general trading.

Table 4-4. Managers' assessments of the contributions of trading companies as partners in joint ventures by stages of development [a]

| | AVERAGE RATING | | | | NORMALIZED RATING | | |
CONTRIBUTION	TOTAL	EARLY	MODERATE	ACTIVE	EARLY	MODERATE	ACTIVE
General knowledge	4.63	5.31	4.82	3.57	0.97	1.45	1.47
Capital and credit	4.23	5.13	4.10	3.36	0.71	0.87	0.85
Government relations	3.86	5.17	3.92	2.19	0.71	0.65	−2.92
Import of raw materials, equipment and machinery	3.78	5.42	3.35	2.11	1.12	0.0	0.37
Marketing policy	3.61	5.21	3.65	2.07	0.12	0.37	0.72
Selection of joint venture partners	3.58	3.72	3.67	3.21	0.72	0.37	0.72
Local logistical support	3.30	4.91	2.67	2.20	0.52	−0.56	−0.51
General management	3.05	4.01	3.02	1.98	−0.42	−0.37	−0.61
Export	0.92	1.07	0.62	1.47	−3.42	−2.62	−0.13

[a] The scales used were as follows: 6 = Very important; 0 = Not important at all.
Early means firms with four joint ventures in manufacturing fewer; Moderate means firms with five to nine joint ventures in manufacturing; Active means firms with ten or more joint ventures in manufacturing.

Table 4-5. Managers' assessments of the conflicts associated with trading companies as partners in joint ventures, by stages of development [a]

AREA OF CONFLICT	AVERAGE RATING				NORMALIZED RATING		
	TOTAL	EARLY	MODERATE	ACTIVE	EARLY	MODERATE	ACTIVE
Source of supply	2.24	1.31	2.15	3.54	0.35	0.44	0.80
Expansion	2.18	1.43	1.95	3.46	0.48	0.20	0.05
Marketing policy	2.11	1.01	2.05	2.61	0.03	0.29	0.24
Transfer price	2.05	0.87	2.20	3.31	−0.08	0.45	0.56
Disposition of earnings	2.04	0.81	2.40	3.00	−0.15	0.15	0.26
Selection of expatriate Japanese executives	1.70	0.69	1.85	2.92	−0.27	0.08	0.18
Financial policy	1.67	0.56	1.10	2.38	−0.31	−0.60	−0.35
Export	1.30	0.68	1.20	2.23	−0.27	−0.55	−0.51
Payment of royalties and fees	1.08	0.44	0.90	2.15	−0.52	−0.85	−0.74

[a] The scales used were as follows: 6 = Very important; 0 = Not important at all.
Early means firms with four joint ventures in manufacturing fewer; Moderate means firms with five to nine joint ventures in manufacturing; Active means firms with ten of more joint ventures in manufacturing.

5. The Manufacturing Firm

Most of the Japanese manufacturing enterprises entered foreign manufacturing activities quite by accident. In the early stages, Japanese enterprises established manufacturing facilities abroad to meet threats to their established market in the countries in question. The initial strategy was to complement the firm's export, and once committed to this course they sought to adopt new strategies to defend their initial position and to exploit further opportunities in the new field.

The commitment to this international strategy required certain adaptations in the structure and operating policies of the Japanese manufacturing enterprises. Specifically, in this analysis I shall focus on organizational responses and changes in the ownership policies of the subsidiaries. Once again, the central concern will be to probe aspects that are uniquely Japanese as well as those that are similar to the developments in U.S.-based multinational enterprise.

For this purpose, I have analyzed the pattern of organizational evolution of the fifty major Japanese manufacturing companies considered particularly active in foreign manufacturing. These companies produced textiles, machinery, transportation equipment, metals, and chemicals. In 1973 they operated 417 manufacturing subsidiaries in 37 countries. Altogether these firms were estimated to account for nearly 40 percent of Japan's direct foreign investment in manufacturing.

Organizational Evolution

A threat to the export market was generally first recognized through normal channels of export, and attempts to counter the threat typically grew out of the way export activities were organized. Thus, in analyzing the evolution of international organiza-

127

tion in Japanese enterprises, it is important to understand how export is conducted, as there are some significant differences between firms using trading companies and those that do not.

Among the types of firm which have exported their products through trading companies are manufacturers of standard commodities such as steel, chemicals, fertilizers, textiles, and the like. For the reasons noted in Chapter 1, trading companies were excellently suited to performing routine export functions for these types of product. However, even manufacturing enterprises that relied on trading companies for export found it necessary to create an export staff to assist the efforts of the trading companies.

One of the critical tasks of the export divisions thus created was to work closely with the trading companies in promoting particular product lines; they supported the trading companies by providing technical services, disseminating information on new products, and arranging for export credit. Internally the export division served as the focal point in promoting the firm's export activities. Its functions included assuring the proper allocation of corporate resources, speedy processing of orders, reliable delivery schedules, and technical adjustments of product requirements. In performing these activities, the export division interacted regularly with other product divisions and staff departments within the corporation.

Another vital function of the export division was planning. In capital intensive industries in particular, advance planning for export was critically important. For most Japanese manufacturers of steel, chemicals, and fibers, export accounted for an important share of their total sales, and it provided the incremental volume to justify the larger scale of operations. Capacity planning in such firms requires a long lead time and a substantial sum of capital. For this purpose, each major export market needs to be carefully examined, important trends ascertained, and major developments anticipated. Since trading companies were typically ill equipped to perform these planning functions for their client manufacturing enterprises, the enterprises found it necessary to develop capabilities of their own for such purposes. To provide technical support and customer services not provided by trading companies, and to gather necessary information, manufacturing enterprises had to go a step further by establishing liaison offices in major export markets.

For these enterprises, it was usually the local representatives of the trading company who first recognized a threat to the company's export market. How the threat was communicated to the manufacturing company was peculiarly Japanese. To comprehend the pattern of this communication, one must have some understanding of the relationship between the manufacturing firm and the trading company. The relationship is not exclusive; a trading company may handle similar products of a number of competing manufacturing companies. Likewise, a manufacturer sells its products through several different trading companies. Considering the nature of the products concerned, the practice makes good sense from the point of view of both the manufacturing and trading companies.

Note that these products are highly standardized and do not readily lend themselves to product differentiation. The ability to match quickly the needs of a company with the supply capabilities of a manufacturing firm is essential. Such products require extensive distribution and wide geographic coverage. The information must be quickly obtained, but the nature of information required is quite simple. Trading companies utilizing their extensive worldwide networks can quickly identify the needs of a particular customer at a particular time with the capabilities of a particular supplier. For this purpose, trading companies have to have multiple suppliers of the same products. With no room for product differentiation, there are no compensating advantages for exclusive representation.

Likewise from the point of view of the manufacturing enterprise, having several trading companies representing it in various parts of the world is advantageous. Understandably, no trading company has the dominant position in every market. Market coverage tends to be uneven. Some trading companies are strong in particular geographic areas or market segments.

Even though the relationship between a manufacturing enterprise and a trading company is not exclusive, there is usually a trading company with which a manufacturing enterprise is particularly close. In most cases, the relationship is based on the traditional Zaibatsu banking ties. For example, Mitsui-related manufacturing firms prefer to deal with Mitsuibusan, and similarly Mitsubishi-based firms have shown a strong preference to work with Mitsubishi Shoji. In cases where the group's trading company was perceived weak in a particular product line or market, competing trading companies have been known to move in to fill the gap. Manufacturing firms tend to encourage such competition among trading companies. Thus, the main trading company for a given manufacturing company could differ among markets.

Since major export markets are served by all leading trading companies, possible restrictions against imports imposed by the host country are recognized by all of them almost simultaneously. Indeed, all major trading companies have extensive information networks to recognize such signals. Moreover, because trading companies deal in a wide variety of products, they have extensive experience in identifying and interpreting such clues. In fact, because of their prior experience and knowledge of the local market, in many cases trading companies are in a position to anticipate in advance possible restrictions. Indeed, the ability to routinize the processing standard and recurring information is a major strength of larger trading companies. Thus, when the local representatives of the trading companies suspect possible import restrictions, they usually move quickly and aggressively to obtain a license to manufacture locally. The host country often offers special inducements to those willing to undertake local production, including incentives and protections to selected firms which meet a set of conditions imposed by the host government. For trading companies, it is critical that they be assured of a local source of supply after import restrictions are imposed. A license to manufacture is a valuable asset in persuading their respective manufacturing companies to establish local plants.

For the first one or two foreign investments of this nature, the initiative rested almost entirely with the trading company. Threatened with the potential loss of an export market, the manufacturing company could hardly reject such a proposal submitted by the trading company with which it was particularly close. The export division of the manufacturing company, preoccupied with managing widespread export operations, was ill suited to planning and implementing such projects. It also lacked the capacity to undertake a careful investigation of the proposed investment. Thus, the export division relied heavily on the trading company for relevant data to prepare a proposal for internal use. The task for preparing the proposal was generally assumed by either the planning group or administrative service staff of the export division working closely with the manager in charge of the particular market.

With a few variations, the same decision-making process applies to manufacturers of end products such as automobiles, electrical appliances, consumer electronics, and the like. Unlike commodities and intermediate materials, successful marketing of these products requires the establishment of enduring relationships with distributors, retail outlets, and most important, customers. Also for these products, marketing programs designed to build product differentiation is extremely important. Trading companies are ill suited to performing these functions, and as the export market developed, manufacturers of these products were compelled to build their own international marketing network. In major markets manufacturers created their own sales subsidiaries. Understandably, when export was threatened, these sales subsidiaries had even stronger vested interests to defend it. Recommendation by the sales subsidiary to undertake local assembly elicited a ready response from the parent company and the suggestion to establish small local assembly facilities was seldom questioned. The sales subsidiary performed most of the preliminary tasks associated with planning for an investment project, including market assessment, search for a local partner, and negotiations with the local government. The export division often sought the assistance of other departments or corporate staff in preliminary negotiations. The engineering staff was brought in for technical consultation; advice of financial experts was sought to determine the financial feasibility of the proposed project. Throughout such a process, the inevitability of the project was emphasized, and the key questions were framed in terms of how the project was to be implemented, rather than its basic wisdom.

Although the manner in which the initial investment opportunities came to the attention of the export division differed, depending on whether or not export was conducted through the trading company or through its own sales subsidiaries, there are several common factors. The threat was first recognized by those close to the market; it was communicated through the organization established for export activities; and the task of planning and implementing a project was assumed by the units located abroad. The export division was rather passive and reactive.

Once created, however, new foreign manufacturing subsidiaries were typically placed under the export division, the logic being that the raison d'être of the foreign manufacturing subsidiaries was to perpetuate export from Japan.

In a Japanese enterprise, at the early stages of the firm's foreign manufacturing, day-to-day operations of the subsidiaries had to be closely controlled by the export division of the parent company. They were considered as part of the firm's export activities. Managers of local subsidiaries had only limited discretion over major decisions, because the subsidiaries were created to complement the firm's export and the major competitive strength of Japanese subsidiaries abroad initially was closely tied to the tremendous economies of scale in production enjoyed by the parent companies in Japan. This is a constrast to the common pattern noted in the early stage of development in U.S.-based multinational enterprises.

Admittedly, the American and Japanese cases do not lend themselves to precise comparison. After all, the multinational evolution of major U.S. enterprises spans at least several decades, nearly a century in some cases. The Japanese case is not only very recent in its evolution, no more than a decade in many cases, but Japanese enterprises are indeed still in the very early stage of development. True, differences in the state of evolution, the timing, and the environment must be carefully taken into account in making a comparison, but the exercise may offer some significant insights. According to Stopford and Wells, the managers of local subsidiaries of American firms had a high degree of autonomy in managing their affairs, which is an aspect of a distinct pattern of multinational expansion of U.S. enterprises. American firms, too, first served foreign markets by means of export. Unlike the Japanese case, however, the major source of competitive advantage for American export lay in innovative technology. In the early phase of the product life cycle, exporting done by American companies with innovative products prospered. But as the local market began to show rapid growth, local producers found ways to manufacture similar products in direct competition with American export. Local producers were usually able to do so at a cost considerably lower than that of the original American manufacturer.

To meet this competition, American firms found it necessary to establish local manufacturing facilities to take advantage of the lower factory costs enjoyed by local competitors. In addition, some American firms found that they could better exploit their brand names by manufacturing locally. For these reasons, American subsidiaries were interested from the beginning in maximizing local production, thus giving local management a high degree of autonomy.

In the case of Japanese firms in the early stages of establishing manufacturing facilities abroad, a purely ad hoc approach to planning worked satisfactorily for the first one or two foreign investment projects. But as the number of projects grew, the need for formalization of assignments became increasingly important. There was a growing recognition that the time-consuming planning required for a new project could not be performed adequately by the already overworked export division planning staff.

Eventually, a small subunit was created, usually within the export division, which specialized in planning for new foreign ventures, marking the first step toward formalization of responsibilities for foreign manufacturing activities. It is important to note here that the group was very much a part of the export division; the chief concern of the new unit was to establish new manufacturing subsidiaries—as extensions of the firm's export activities. The management of existing subsidiaries was still as a rule under the control of the line managers of the export division.

The formation of these subunits took place quite early in the development of international business activities of the Japanese manufacturing firms studied. By 1973, in forty-six of the fifty enterprises studied, planning staffs had been created. Moreover, in all these firms, the unit came into being within ten years of the creation of the first manufacturing subsidiary. Also, in thirty-six firms—almost 80 percent of those studied—the creation of the international staff came about by the time the company had four manufacturing subsidiaries abroad.

Creating an International Division

In Chapter 3, I noted that Japanese manufacturing activities abroad had been concentrated in mature industries and they soon came under intensive competitive pressure. To arrest the tide of rapidly eroding competitive advantages, Japanese enterprises began to adopt new strategies—strategies that had become quite familiar in U.S.-based multinational enterprises in mature oligopolies. These strategies included: upgrading and broadening product lines; emphasizing product differentiation through marketing means; and achieving vertical integration.

As the subsidiaries began to pursue these strategies, their character underwent a gradual, rather subtle, change. For one thing, the subsidiaries required a commitment of new resources from the corporate headquarters. Adding new products, adopting new promotional techniques, and particularly seeking greater vertical integration required the inputs of new technologies, the infusion of additional capital, and often the assignment of new technical or engineering personnel from the parent company. The managers in the export division, however, were not well equipped to intercede on behalf of the struggling subsidiaries for mobilizing resources of the parent company. Preoccupied with day-to-day operations involving many different markets throughout the world, the export division was observed to be less than sympathetic to the needs of the new subsidiaries. The export division possessed few of the required resources itself. For example, in the case of financing, the export division had considerable funds at its disposal for financing export to foreign subsidiaries as a part of normal trade. In fact, much of the working capital used by foreign subsidiaries was in the form of trade credit extended either by the parent company or the trading companies with which it dealt. The export division, however, was not typically in a position to provide the foreign subsidiaries with funds needed for building new production facilities. New capital appropriations had to be sought. This meant that the export division had to sponsor a proposal for new capital appropriations and submit it to relevant groups at the corporate headquarters. This was and is a time-consuming and complicated process even under the ideal circumstances. The matter is complicated by distance and a lack of familiarity with the local conditions. The enthusiasm of the export division would be further dampened by the fact that in most cases the proposed appropriation would be spent for building local production facilities leading to greater self-sufficiency on the part of the subsidiaries and in the reduction of export from the parent company.

Moreover, the export division did not possess the needed technologies. They had to be obtained either from the product division or a plant. The product divisions were seldom interested in extending assistance to small struggling foreign subsidiaries. Managers of large domestic divisions or plants found it impossible to understand the problems faced by the managers of foreign subsidiaries in their desperate efforts to shore up their competitive strength. It was even more difficult for the foreign subsidiaries to persuade the corporate staff and the product divisions to send qualified personnel to implement the new strategies. The product divisions and plants were usually not eager to send their most qualified managers and technicians to small subsidiaries abroad.

Disappointed with the lack of support from line managers in the export division, the managers of the subsidiaries gradually began to urge strengthening the small international business groups to assume responsibilities beyond planning new ventures, and to have the group take on new functions of servicing the needs of existing subsidiaries. The staff, though small and limited, was more sympathetic to the needs of the subsidiaries. The staff was not involved in day-to-day operations, and it had by this time come to the realization that the needs of the subsidiaries, once created, were often neglected. Understandably, the staff was particularly sensitive to the needs of those subsidiaries which they had a hand in creating. The staff was also most anxious to expand its sphere of influence to include coordinating the affairs of the existing subsidiaries. The international staff also became aware of the growing conflict between the export division and the foreign manufacturing subsidiaries as the latter began to pursue an independent course of action.

Partly because of these situations and also in response to potential opportunities for growth of foreign manufacturing activities, the international staff sought to break out of its earlier mold and began to seek an independent divisional status. To justify a higher status for itself, the international staff cited a number of justifications. One was an argument that the character of foreign manufacturing subsidiaries had changed and that it was no longer enough to view them merely as an extension of export operations. The international staff argued that at initial stages the operations of the subsidiaries were so closely tied to export that there were many advantages in having them controlled closely by the export division. Moreover, at this stage, the performance of the subsidiaries was not terribly important as long as the transfer price of the export from the parent company was closely controlled. But as the subsidiaries pursued new strategies, and as the requirement for resources at the subsidiaries increased, and as much of the production began to take place locally, export from Japan was reduced to a minimum. In the face of these developments, the international staff argued that it was increasingly important to watch closely the performance of the local subsidiaries. They were quick to point out that these functions could not be performed adequately by line managers of the export division and, in fact, they argued convincingly that as long as the foreign subsidiaries were in the export division, their long-term welfare would be impaired. Also by this time, the international staff had gained sufficient capabilities of its own to provide useful support for the subsidiaries. By this time, having been exposed to a variety of problems encountered by different subsidiaries, the international staff was able to handle many recurring problems without referring them to other corporate groups. The staff could not anticipate many of the problems. Even in cases where outside assistance was needed, the international staff was now able to interpret the request of the subsidiaries to other groups at the parent company and to elicit appropriate responses. In a number of firms, these developments coincided with the replacement of the original team of managers by new ones. These men, inexperienced in international business, eagerly looked to the international staff for information, guidance, and support.

In this process, the international staff in a number of the firms studied successfully transformed itself from a staff attached to the export division to full-fledged divisional status, equal at least in formal structure to other divisions, including the export division. In thirty-four of the fifty firms, the international staff had achieved the independent divisional status within ten years of the establishment of the first manufacturing subsidiary abroad.

The international division then became the profit center for foreign manufacturing activities. The struggle for the international staff to break out of the dominant export division was an important phenomenon for Japanese enterprises; such a need was felt much less keenly, if at all, by U.S.-based multinational enterprises because for them, export had been relatively unimportant. In contrast, in the Japanese case, most of the firms which established foreign subsidiaries were those that were particularly active in exporting. For example, among the fifty companies, the percentage of export to the total sales ranged from 10 to 40 percent, averaging slightly higher than 25 percent. It is readily understandable that in these enterprises, the export division occupied a pivotal position. This was in striking contrast to American multinational enterprises in their early stages of development where the export staff was typically relegated to a minor position and its functions were often absorbed when the international division was created. Even if the export division were allowed to maintain its identity, it was rarely strong enough to challenge the international division. In Japanese manufacturing enterprises, however, the international staff had to achieve its own legitimacy and identity in the shadow of the extremely powerful export division. As it struggled to grow out of the influence of the export division, tensions developed between the two.

Strengthening the International Division

As I have shown in Chapter 3, strategies designed to arrest the erosion of competitive ability seldom proved effective over the long run. Much to their disappointment, most Japanese firms learned that competitive advantages gained through such means as broadening product lines, product differentiation, and even vertical integration proved only temporary. Such a realization, coupled with increasingly competent international divisions, prompted some of the aggressive firms to seek new strategies.

One major strategy was to build large enough production facilities abroad to give the operation a sufficient economy of scale. Having recognized the vulnerability of small manufacturing facilities, a few of the firms began to build sufficiently large manufacturing facilities at a small number of selected sites. These facilities were designed to manufacture intermediate materials or to engage in integrated operations from manufacturing of parts and components to assembly of finished products. In synthetic fibers I have cited examples of the leading firms in the manufacturing of basic raw materials. Similarly, a few of the leading manufacturers of consumer electronics began to build major integrated manufacturing facilities in a few selected countries. To create large-scale facilities, particularly in developing countries where the size of the domestic market was limited, it was necessary that these major facilities be linked with the company's operations located elsewhere.

The pursuit of these strategies created new managerial tasks. First, because of the substantial commitment of corporate resources and the risks associated with such investments, planning and prior investigation became more important than was the case with initial investments. Such a need led to the emergence of a new subunit within the international division: a group specializing in planning, whose responsibilities involved identifying new opportunities, undertaking feasibility studies, and negotiating with the host government and potential partners. In planning a major project, the unit became the focal point among various corporate staff groups, including the finance, technical unit, marketing and personnel departments in coordinating the project. Because of the size of the investment and risks involved, the task for lobbying and promoting the project within the parent company was at times quite difficult. The planning task became further complicated by the fact that large-scale investments were designed to serve more than one market. The demand in other markets had to be estimated, the usual uncertainties associated with export to these markets had to be assessed, and of course, such a project had to be coordinated with future plans of those subsidiaries which the new facilities would serve.

How difficult and time-consuming are the negotiations and problems associated with planning a major new venture is illustrated in the attempt of a major synthetic fiber manufacturer to establish a fiber plant in Thailand. To plan and implement this project, the international division organized a task force, pooling experts from relevant groups throughout the company. Teams were dispatched to undertake feasibility studies. The task force took the initiative in obtaining favorable terms of entry from the local government. These terms included a ban on the importation of polyester fiber of the type to be manufactured inside Thailand by the company. They also included guarantees as to repatriation of profit, allocation of foreign exchange for the import of necessary machinery, work permits for Japanese managers, and so on. Key managers and technical personnel for the subsidiary were selected with care and well in advance of the beginning of operations. In this process, the task force deliberately departed from the past practice of sending managers with limited capacities and future promise. After much internal recruiting and negotiating, it succeeded in persuading one of the firm's most promising upper-middle managers to head the new operation.

The task force also took pains to recruit qualified local personnel—engineers, technicians, and supervisors. Some of them were sent to Japan several months prior to the time when local operations were to begin and, whenever possible, were trained by the Japanese managers and engineers who had been selected to go to Thailand.

Because the subsidiary was to manufacture the home raw material and to replace the export, the manufacturing company was anxious to obtain the majority ownership. Trading companies were excluded from equity participation despite their intense efforts to become involved. The international division concluded that the trading companies had little to contribute to such an operation, and the firm was anxious not to dilute its ownership.

In addition to planning functions, the commitment to these strategies required certain managerial tasks, that is, closer control and coordination of the subsidiaries by the international division. When the firm's international operations were confined to a small import-substitution type of investment, control did not pose much of a problem. In contrast, for new major manufacturing subsidiaries, the capital commitment was large and export from the parent company was substantially reduced if not totally replaced. The performance of the subsidiaries became an important concern to the parent company, particularly to the international division, which by this time had come to assume profit responsibility for the firm's international operations.

To achieve system-wide benefits, regular communication between the parent company and the subsidiaries was necessary. This need for close control and coordination resulted in another structural change within the international division—the establishment of the area staff. Within the international division, the world was broken up into several major regions, and a small staff was assigned to each area. These men, some of whom had served at the subsidiary level, had acquired substantial area knowledge which facilitated further close communication between the parent company and the subsidiaries. In a few cases, the area or regional management centers were located in a particular region instead of in Japan.

Along with these structural changes the international division sought to establish a formal system of information collection. For example, in one leading firm, each subsidiary submitted a standard set of reports every month to the international division, including a balance sheet, profit and loss statement, cash flow statement, and a report on marketing, manufacturing, and personnel. These reports, dealing with various aspects of the subsidiary's operations, were accompanied by a narrative report presenting major political and economic developments in the country during the period covered. These reports were carefully scrutinized by the staff in the international division responsible for a particular area. In this process, deviations from the budget were spotted and abnormal patterns singled out for immediate attention.

The primary purpose of the monthly review was to serve as an early warning system. Every quarter, the performances of the subsidiaries were evaluated by a five-man formal review committee, consisting of the heads of the international division, export division, corporate planning staff, engineering department, and finance department. The inclusion of these important executives was believed to add weight to the review process and, at the same time, to keep the executives informed of the company's international activities. For this review, the international division made a comparative analysis of the performance of the individual subsidiaries. The international division also prepared a formal report to the executive committee and to the board every three months.

Still another major structural change in the international division at this stage was the creation of a staff charged with international financial functions. The commitment to the new strategies resulted in substantial capital commitments for foreign manufacturing activities, which in turn necessitated closer financial planning and control. In earlier investments, the fund to be committed was small and credit was to be extended by the parent company, or else the trading companies, in connection with export of intermediate materials or parts, provided an important source of financing. As a result, the firms gave little systematic attention to central financial planning and coordination. In essence, these firms were in a situation analogous to the Phase I postulated by Robbins and Stobaugh.[1] The rapid increase in capital requirement of firms committed to the strategy of major international expansion programs can be illustrated by the following example of one such firm.

At the end of 1973 the company's total financial commitment in foreign affiliates in the forms of investment and long-term loans exceeded $74 million. The projects in the summer of 1974, when completed, were expected to raise the cumulative total to $110 million. If short-term and medium-term credit extended by the parent company and loans obtained from financial institutions with the parent company's guarantee were included, the total would be considerably larger.

Such rapid growth of capital requirements prompted these firms to give closer attention to international financial management. No longer was it practical, as in the past, to rely solely on Japanese sources for financing foreign ventures, and the firms were increasingly compelled to tap the international money markets. These firms began to develop links with U.S. and European multinational financial institutions. Also, with much higher stakes abroad, the firms began to recognize some of the potential benefits of system-wide integration in financial management. Systematic attempts to manage flows of funds among the subsidiaries began. Thus, a few firms entered the early stage of Phase II in the evolution of financial management, as postulated by Robbins and Stobaugh. To perform these functions several firms in my sample of fifty established a small staff in the international division, charged with financial management. Some established a finance company outside Japan to raise funds overseas and to coordinate the flow of funds among various subsidiaries. For example, in 1973 Toshiba established a wholly-owned finance company in the Netherlands. Its first assignment was to raise $9 million abroad to help finance the company's wholly-owned semiconductor plant in Malaysia.

In the mid-1970s only a handful of Japanese manufacturing enterprises had begun to attain the kind of maturity described here. With the growing importance of foreign manufacturing activities, planning and control functions were stressed. With replacement of export, profit responsibility of the international division was sharpened and reporting procedures became formalized.

These developments had rather close parallel in the evolution of the international division in U.S.-based multinational enterprises. Stopford and Wells note that when the international division was established, a move toward centralization occurred and a formal planning and control system was adopted. The task of planning and coordination was directed toward raising the overall performance above the level that would be possible if each subsidiary behaved autonomously. The possibilities of realizing substantial economic gains from coordination of the foreign subsidiaries provided pressure for centralizing decision making within the international division.

In Japanese multinational enterprises, the speed with which such concentration took place appeared to be considerably faster. This was because of the high concentration of Japanese multinationals in standard products and mature technologies.

In the behavior of the international division at this stage of development two important differences are to be noted between U.S. and Japanese multinational enterprises. In the Japanese case, a very powerful export division continued to exist along with the international division. Because of the importance of export, the division is too powerful to be absorbed by the international division. The only major step toward achieving some sort of coordination between the export and international division would be to have the heads of both the export and international divisions report to the same managing director. This practice is followed by a number of major Japanese firms. The other difference is that the activities of the international division in U.S. multinational enterprises are seldom closely monitored by the central office of the enterprise. International business is self-contained and is managed by an autonomous division independent of the rest of the corporation. In contrast, in Japanese enterprises where the best tradition of the Ringi system (see Chapter 6) prevails, the responsibilities of the managers are ill defined and each major decision must be acted on as it occurs. A proposal submitted by one group is examined both formally and informally by managers in a number of key positions. In this process, de facto corporate-wide integration takes place. The international division, like other product divisions and staff groups, is very much a part of this process. As a result, it is essential for the international division to maintain constant communication with the rest of the corporation. Thus, the international division in a Japanese multinational enterprise appears to be much less autonomous and independent than its American counterpart.

Strategy and Ownership Policy

We have seen how Japan's major manufacturing enterprises adopted a new organizational structure in response to changing international strategies. In this analysis I have shown an increasing trend toward tighter controls by the international division over the activities of the subsidiaries. Another aspect of control is the ownership policy of the subsidiaries. In this aspect, there is a striking contrast between Japanese- and U.S.-based multinational enterprises. A recent study of international activities of Japanese enterprises undertaken by the Ministry of International Trade and Industry reported that of 661 major manufacturing firms surveyed, in over a half of them, the Japanese parent companies held only a minority position. The majority- or wholly-owned Japanese subsidiaries accounted for less than a quarter of the total number of subsidiaries. Although not directly comparable, nearly two thirds of the subsidiaries of the 177 leading U.S. multinational enterprises were majority- or wholly-owned.

Why does such a difference exist in the ownership of the subsidiaries of multinational enterprises of two different national origins? My study suggests that this is due largely to different strategies pursued by U.S.- and Japan-based multinational enterprises. The study has also shown that as Japanese manufacturing enterprises began to pursue strategies similar to those of U.S.-based multinational enterprises, they too began to manifest a definite preference for control.

Import Substitution Strategy

There is pervasive evidence that while Japanese manufacturing firms pursued the strategy of import substitution, they did not consider absolute control of their subsidiaries important. This is borne out by data collected from the same fifty Japanese manufacturing enterprises which constituted the sample for the analysis presented in the last section. These enterprises had a total of 417 subsidiaries, of which 342, or roughly 82 percent, were joint ventures, and of the 342 joint ventures, in 304 the Japanese parent companies owned 50 percent or less.

Detailed examination of these joint ventures indicates that most of them were created for the purpose of defending the export market. They were typically very small, depended heavily on the parent company for intermediate materials or components, and served only the local market. Of the 304 manufacturing subsidiaries, 46 percent were capitalized at less than 100 million, or $333,000. Nearly 44 percent fell in the range of 100 million to 1 billion, or $333,000 to $3.3 million. Judging from the size of the total amount of capital invested, one can see that they were designed only to perform rather limited manufacturing or assembly activities. The strategy of the parent company was clearly to maximize export from Japan to these subsidiaries, as is readily apparent in Table 5-1. Except for one industry, the subsidiaries obtained from one third to three quarters of their materials or parts from the parent companies. The one exception is the paper and pulp industry, in which the subsidiaries were designed to perform some processing at the source, before their output was shipped to Japan. These investments were quite different from the others in that they were made in order to supply the Japanese domestic market. Also, as can be seen in Table 5-2, most investments in joint ventures sold their output exclusively in the local markets.

It is true that the import substitution type of investment was heavily concentrated in host countries where local ownership was required as a condition of entry. As long as Japanese manufacturing companies pursued this strategy, the requirement for local ownership was not a deterrent for entry. The enterprises were interested in obtaining only a sufficient degree of control to defend the local market for the export of intermediate materials and parts. Because the subsidiaries were designed to manufacture for and sell exclusively to the local market, there were no potentially thorny problems regarding coordination among joint ventures for export to third countries. Moreover, since the technology employed by these subsidiaries was mature and widely diffused and only limited production was performed by these firms, there was little need for protecting proprietary know-how. Moreover, the lack of experience and knowledge of foreign manufacturing operations also made Japanese companies more cautious about committing a large amount of capital. Joint ventures, at least as they were perceived, reduced such a risk.

There is yet another reason for the preference of joint ventures by Japanese manufacturing firms pursuing this particular strategy. Many of the Japanese firms faced threats to their exports simultaneously in a number of countries and found it necessary to respond to these threats if they were to defend their positions. The joint venture approach helped these companies spread their scarce resources over a number of markets with a minimum of time lag. The need to create as many captive outlets as possible was particularly strong among the manufacturers of intermediate materials. Intermediate materials such as synthetic fibers, chemicals, petrochemicals, and iron sheets or rods were used for manufacturing a wide variety of end products. It was important, therefore, for these manufacturers to create captive users of their materials in different industries. Through the means of joint ventures, Japanese manufacturing firms were able to obtain a sufficient degree of control with a minimum of investment to establish a captive supply relationship. The imposition by foreign countries of import restrictions on end products quickly led to the emergence of local firms manufacturing these products. They were small-scale units, performing labor intensive operations using simple technology, and the Japanese suppliers found it advantageous to create captive users of their raw or intermediate materials for as many major product lines as possible.

Assuring Raw Materials

Another group of Japanese firms has consistently followed a joint venture policy. These are firms pursuing a strategy of vertical integration in which joint ventures are used to assure the access to raw material. This can be seen, for example, in the Japanese paper and pulp industry. With only limited domestic resources, Japanese paper manufacturers established joint ventures with major suppliers of pulp, notably in North America. The strategy here was to obtain only the degree of ownership necessary for the Japanese manufacturers to gain guaranteed access to raw materials at a reasonable cost. This enabled them to build the barriers of entry for paper manufacturing through vertical integration. The joint venture approach was also consistent with the desire of foreign suppliers to obtain long-term captive users of raw materials. Of the 13 percent of the subsidiaries which sold less than half of their output in the local market, about one third represented Japanese investments in pulp, where the entire output was imported to Japan after initial processing at the source.

Another example of this strategy is found in the petrochemical and chemical industries. For example, the contemplated Japanese petrochemical project in Iran would have the National Iranian Oil as partner at the crude oil stage in order to assure the project a captive supplier of the critical raw material. Likewise, Teijin's proposed chemical plant in Indonesia was to have Pertermina, the country's national oil company, as its partner, and for the same reason.

Rationalization of Production

Because joint ventures are so prevalent among Japanese foreign manufacturing subsidiaries, it is particularly noteworthy that the fifty firms in our sample had 75 wholly-owned subsidiaries. The analysis of these wholly-owned subsidiaries is revealing, for it points to the fact that for certain types of investment, Japanese companies sought absolute control. Of the 75 wholly-owned subsidiaries, 52, or roughly 70 percent were so-called offshore production facilities designed to export their total output to other markets.

As noted in Chapter 3, offshore investments, particularly in consumer electronics, were made as a defensive action against the move by American competitors to low-wage countries to manufacture or assemble inexpensive consumer electronics products. As the Japanese manufacturers experienced a rapid erosion of competitive strength of their export position in the United States, they too turned to a strategy of rationalization of production. One such approach was to shift production of the lower end of the standard product lines to low-wage countries. There were several reasons why 100 percent ownership was desirable in pursuing this strategy. First, in an industry characterized by intense competition, assurance of the quality of the products manufactured or assembled in offshore facilities was considered critically important. This was particularly the case for Japanese manufacturers because prospective American buyers had lingering uncertainties about the quality of Japanese products.

Second, since the entire output was to be sold in a third market, there was a particularly great need for close coordination among the several units within the Japanese firm. Because of the shifting requirements of the market and the changing levels of capacity utilization at the Japanese plants, the parent company found it necessary to make frequent changes in the product mix to be manufactured by offshore facilities. The situation was further complicated by the fact that Japanese manufacturers sold their products to different distributors and mass merchandising firms to be marketed under their own brands. Such a practice necessitated frequent adjustments in the types and models of products to be manufactured by the offshore facilities to satisfy different customer requirements. The companies were understandably anxious to make their decisions without being hampered by local partners.

A third factor favoring management control for offshore facilities was the manufacturers' desire to maintain some degree of flexibility in determining the transfer prices of parts and components shipped to, as well as from, the offshore facilities as assembled products. Major components and parts were shipped to these plants from Japan, particularly at the early stage of their operations, and finished products were distributed through the companies' wholly-owned subsidiaries in a third market. Under these circumstances, there were considerable advantages to the company in being able to determine the transfer price at its discretion. The presence of local partners would be likely to limit this flexibility, since they would be anxious to obtain the lowest possible transfer price to assure the highest profit to be accrued to the subsidiary.

A number of developing countries offered incentives of various sorts to foreign enterprises interested in creating offshore manufacturing facilities. Often included among the incentives was the exemption of foreign investors from the usual requirement of local ownership. Moreover, for offshore facilities, potential benefits of having local partners were limited. For example, government contacts and general knowledge of the local environment, often representing the areas of major contributors, were less critical in offshore operations. Because of their ability to provide exports to the host country, offshore facilities tended to have a strong bargaining position with the local government. Moreover, the offshore plants were usually located in a specially designed zone where the government offered various programs to facilitate operations of the foreign firms, such as central recruiting and dormitory facilities for workers and simplified procedures for customs clearance. These special facilities tended to reduce the need for local knowledge of partners. Also, since the total output was for export, there was no need for local partners' contributions in the area of marketing.

Changing Strategies and Ownership Policies

As I have shown in Chapter 3, during a relatively short period of time, the strategies of Japanese enterprises regarding their foreign manufacturing activities underwent considerable change. Stopford and Wells concluded from their extensive study of U.S. multinational enterprises that firms pursuing different strategies tended to follow different ownership policies.

In another study, Lawrence Franko noted that changes in strategies of the multinational enterprises resulted in corresponding alterations in their ownership policies. Franko noted that of some 1,000 joint ventures of U.S. multinational enterprises which he examined, 315 had at some time experienced major changes in ownership. He found that joint ventures were most prone to instability in ownership when certain explicit changes took place in the parent company's strategy.[2] Franko noted that as an enterprise began to pursue the strategies that emphasized tighter control over their subsidiaries, they tended to change their minority control, or to buy out their partner's interests altogether. In the case of joint ventures where neither alternative was feasible, they often chose to divest themselves of their holdings. Franko demonstrated that the instability of joint ventures peaked within two years after changes in the strategies had taken place in the parent firm. Franko also found that changes in strategy led to alterations in the firm's attitude toward new joint ventures. After the changes in their strategies took place, their propensity to enter new joint ventures typically declined in the decade following the change. Thus, changes in strategy requiring greater control led these enterprises to reassess the costs and benefits of existing joint ventures and to adjust their policies toward new ones.

Though the Japanese experience is limited and is of recent origin, the available data do point to the presence of certain patterns of relationships between strategies and ownership policies. To obtain an initial clue, I sought the views of the senior international managers of 150 major Japanese manufacturing enterprises regarding the benefits and costs associated with joint ventures. The sample was selected from firms which were listed in the Tokyo Stock Exchange and which had at least two manufacturing joint ventures abroad. The respondents were asked to give an overall evaluation of their experiences regarding their joint ventures. The managers were asked to rank the importance on nine kinds of contributions made by their local partners in their foreign manufacturing ventures. Each factor was ranked on a descending scale from 6 (extremely important) to 0 (not important at all). Similarly, the managers were asked to rank the relative importance of the eleven possible areas of conflict.

Responses were received from 87 firms. As a crude measure of changes in strategy, the 87 companies were categorized into three groups according to the number of manufacturing subsidiaries that were operating at the time of the survey—the early stage (5 or fewer), the moderately active stage (6-14), and the active stage (15 or more). To provide a basis for comparative analysis, each firm needed to be classified according to its perceptions of the relative importance of the different benefits and problems. For this purpose, some adjustments had to be made to the responses. In effect, each firm had to be classified on the basis of the sequences in which it ordered the various contributions or problems, not on the basis of the actual number that it assigned to the importance.

Consider the following example. Firm *A* evaluated all contributions as 2 except for capital which it gave the rating of 4; Firm *B* gave the rating of 6 to everything else but capital, to which it assigned 4. If the simple averages of the two firms are compared, both would be 4, but relative to other contributions the Firm *A* clearly ranks capital higher than Firm *B*. This difference is highlighted by the normalization process.

$$\text{Firm } A \qquad 4 - \frac{4 + (8 \times 2)}{9} = 1.78$$

$$\text{Firm } B \qquad 4 - \frac{4 + (8 \times 6)}{9} = -1.77$$

The normalized values for contributions of local partners and conflicts experienced with each are presented in Tables 5-3 and 5-4. To probe further reasons for particular responses, personal interviews were conducted with managers of key firms.

The managers of enterprises in the early stage of international growth gave relatively high ratings to those contributions of the partners which related to the local environment. At these stages, the managers, keenly aware of their own unfamiliarity with the foreign environment, valued the partner's knowledge and experience in this regard. This stage is relatively free from tension. Small subsidiaries performing limited operations required few major decisions. Moreover, since they were considered merely an extension of the firm's export strategy, little was expected from them. At this stage, the parent company often made its resources available to the joint venture quite generously through informal channels.

There is one notable exception to this general absence of tension. This concerns the issue of transfer price. Because at this stage the joint ventures were heavily dependent on the Japanese parent company for supplies of materials and components, it is readily understandable that the decision regarding transfer price would be a frequent source of conflict.

By the time the parent companies reached the moderately active stage, they had established an international division, and some had begun to pursue a strategy of actively expanding the number of subsidiaries. The international staff, however, was still quite small and limited in competence. Faced with the pressure for rapid expansion and with limited resources for foreign manufacturing, they valued contributions of local partners that tended to facilitate expansion. In ranking the contributions of their local partners, the managers of the enterprises in this stage attributed the highest importance to those factors relating to the local government's knowledge of the environment, government relations, and local managerial practices, particularly those concerned with labor relations. As in the early stage, the parent company expected little from the local partners in such areas as capital, technology, marketing, and access to raw materials.

While transfer price was an important point of conflict at this stage, other sources of tension began to arise as well, especially with regard to the disposition of earnings, the pricing of the output of joint ventures, the selection of Japanese expatriate executives, and the uses of the Japanese manufacturer's brand.

By this time, some of the subsidiaries had become profitable and it became necessary for the partners to deal with the disposition of the profits. A frequent source of friction was that local partners often want immediate distribution of the profit. As a matter of fact, the disposition of earnings often brought out the fundamental differences in the partners' expectations of the venture, differences that had been hidden during the earlier phases of development.

Also at this stage, the expatriate managers assigned to the local subsidiary became a focus of conflict. By this time, having had several years of experience with a substantial number of Japanese executives, local partners became quite concerned, with some justification, over the high cost associated with supporting Japanese expatriates. To make matters worse, the managers were not always carefully chosen. As is often the case in domestic subsidiaries, managers assigned to small foreign affiliates were usually either individuals with limited potential or those nearing retirement. Complaints concerning the poor caliber of Japanese expatriates were often heard from the local partners. They were also concerned over the frequent turnover of these executives.

Another serious source of tension at this stage was found to be the determination of the price at which the output of the joint venture was to be sold, a problem which was particularly acute when one of the partners controlled marketing, and the manufacturing subsidiary had in effect become the captive supplier to the sales outlets controlled by one of the partners. For example, in the home appliance industry, the Japanese partner already had a wholly-owned sales subsidiary established at the export stage, through which the entire output of the manufacturing joint venture was to be sold. Pricing of the output of the joint venture became particularly troublesome, as some of the subsidiaries began to experience the full rigor of competition in the local market, along with the erosion of their initial oligopolistic advantages. Faced with the pressure of price cutting, the partner controlling marketing in turn applied pressure on the manufacturing joint venture to lower its price over stiff opposition of the other partners.

Let us now look at firms in the third stage of development, that is, companies which were internationally active. By this stage, most firms were firmly committed to regain competitive advantages. In doing so, it became apparent to Japanese enterprises that they could hardly rely on local partners for financial, technical, and managerial resources. Local partners were often found to be either unable or unwilling to provide these resources. The difficulties were increased by the fact that the local partners of the Japanese ventures were dominated by relatively small businessmen. This is evident from a random sampling of 100 firms selected from the 342 joint ventures owned by the fifty major enterprises. These 100 joint ventures had a total of 361 local partners, each of whom held at least 5 percent equity in one of the ventures. The backgrounds of the partners fell into the following categories:

Individuals (including closely held family corporations)		305
Entrepreneurs engaged in manufacturing	102	
Entrepreneurs engaged primarily in commerce	119	
Individuals engaged primarily in service industries other than commerce	39	
Individuals not in any of the above activities	45	
Publicly held corporations		32
Government or quasi-government organizations		24
Total	305	361

These data demonstrate the dominance of individual entrepreneurs in particular as partners in Japanese manufacturing joint ventures abroad. Understandably, most of them had only limited resources, and the majority of the entrepreneurs had been engaged primarily in commercial activities which emphasized short term returns.

A number of firms at this stage also sought to recapture the initial advantages through emphasizing product differentiation. Local partners did not always appreciate the potential value of such strategies and resisted allocating additional resources for such a purpose. Moreover, only the Japanese partners had the expertise necessary to assume leadership over the local marketing operations of the local subsidiaries, which were often neglected by local partners in implementing these strategies. For these reasons, marketing was singled out as the serious area of conflict by the managers of the firms in the final stage of development.

Expansion of local production facilities also became an important source of conflict. In undertaking these expansions, it was not uncommon for Japanese parent companies to provide many of the resources needed. For example, in enlarging the equity base of the subsidiary, Japanese companies have been known to loan the needed funds to local partners for use as their contribution in order to maintain the outward appearance of joint ventures. A heavy infusion of managerial and technological resources was made by the Japanese parent companies. All these actions altered the relationship between the partners. Typically, in return for resources they provided, Japanese partners asserted themselves strongly in the management of joint ventures.

Local partners also objected to attempts by Japanese partners to gain system-wide benefits through coordinating the activities of various subsidiaries. Local partners felt that such advantages accrued largely to the Japanese parent companies. They also feared possible loss of their bargaining power vis-à-vis their Japanese partners by letting the joint ventures become integrated into the large multinationally integrated companies.

Decisions must be made concerning the location of production and sourcing of various components within the corporate system and, of course, concerning the transfer price to be charged for such intracompany transactions. These decisions had to be made at a higher level than the subsidiaries and required a high degree of centralization at the headquarters.

Japanese firms whose strength is based largely on economies of scale begin to show a preference for unequivocal control once they become committed in earnest to the strategy of rationalization of production. The pursuit of this strategy requires close control and coordination among the subsidiaries, which can be best achieved by 100 percent ownership. The commitment to this strategy is most evident in the consumer electronics industry, an industry characterized by intense competition and by significant economies of scale.

Toshiba, Matsushita, and Hitachi—three leading firms—established in 1974 major manufacturing facilities in Malaysia to supply certain standard components to other foreign subsidiaries. For these subsidiaries, which were to become an integrated element in the parent company's logistical system, unambiguous control was considered critically important.

Stopford and Wells have reported from their study of the ownership policy of U.S.-based multinational enterprises that the firms whose oligopolistic advantages were based on marketing tend to seek 100 percent control of their subsidiaries. They do so for two reasons: the ready availability of marketing skills within the firm; and the commitment to a given marketing strategy. These firms, the authors noted, possess strong marketing expertise, and moreover central control over the marketing activities of the subsidiaries was critical to the success of the strategy of the firm. To date, only a small number of firms entered foreign markets successfully on the strength of marketing. Though the evidence is far from conclusive, it appears that the Japanese multinational firms which are seemingly committed to this strategy have a preference for 100 percent ownership of their subsidiaries. (See Table 5.5.) Some of the leading Japanese manufacturers of consumer durables have successfully built product differentiation in their export markets, particularly in the United States. Matsushita and Sony in consumer electronics and Kawasaki in motorcycles are notable cases in point. Where some of these firms faced a sufficient threat to their export position, they responded by creating their own manufacturing facilities in major export markets including the United States. Anxious to continue to exploit the brand names established at the export stage, they preferred 100 percent ownership of their subsidiaries. Through export, these firms had acquired substantial knowledge of the local environment and the industry. With outstanding technical capacities, strong market positions, ready access to the capital resources, and excellent knowledge of the local environment, they had little need for local partners. Moreover, 100 percent ownership would give the parent company freedom to coordinate the manufacturing policy between the domestic and foreign plants.

Stopford and Wells also demonstrated that the U.S.-based multinational enterprises which follow a strategy of continuous generation of new products have shown a strong preference for 100 percent ownership for several reasons. For one thing, such U.S. enterprises find it difficult to arrive at arrangements with local partners that provide what they consider to be a fair return for the technology they contribute. Equally important is their concern for technology. IBM is a classic example of a U.S.-based multinational enterprise that has followed the strategy of 100 percent ownership.

There have been few Japanese manufacturing investments which derived their primary competitive advantages from technology. Once again, the evidence is highly tentative. But one or two enterprises that could fall into this category seem to prefer 100 percent ownership of their manufacturing subsidiaries. Sony is one such firm. Though a good part of the company's strength is derived from its marketing, its success is due in part to its ability to generate a succession of innovative products. True, Sony's technologies do not represent fundamental innovation. However, they are sufficiently substantial to give the firm a significant, albeit temporary, advantage. The company has established 100 percent owned sales subsidiaries in many export markets through which it administers centrally controlled, standard-marketing programs. As the company turned to the creation of manufacturing subsidiaries abroad, it was aware of the importance of protecting its technology and the need to assure smooth transfer of products from the parent company to its manufacturing subsidiaries abroad. These considerations placed a high premium on control over foreign manufacturing affiliates. Also, given the depth and breadth of knowledge of foreign markets possessed by the company, 100 percent ownership promised greater benefits than the additional resources a potential partner could bring to a joint venture. As these enterprises become committed to new strategies, it becomes quite evident that the managers' erstwhile preference for joint venture has undergone a significant change.

In the survey referred to earlier, the managers were asked to consider majority ownership of their foreign manufacturing subsidiaries. The composition of these enterprises was particularly revealing. As many as 16 of them had at least 15 manufacturing subsidiaries. Therefore they fell in my category of internationally active firms. The remaining three fell among the moderately successful group. Significantly, none of the firms in the early stage of international growth considered majority control important. Moreover, 11 of the 16 in the third stage and 2 of the 3 in the second stage were manufacturers of consumer-related products such as textiles, automobiles, home appliances, and consumer electronics. The 19 firms which considered majority ownership important gave the following reasons:

Relative importance of reasons for desiring
majority control of foreign manufacturing affiliates

Reasons	Mean score of answers
To maintain quality standard	4.68
To protect company brand names	4.32
To protect the company's technology	3.84
To coordinate export	3.00
To control dividend policy	2.95
To integrate production	2.58
To standardize marketing	2.52
To integrate financial management	1.58

The first three factors deal with protection of the parent company's distinctive assets—quality of products, brands, and technology. Even among these firms, less importance was attached to issues of operational integration, such as coordination of export and rationalization of production among subsidiaries.

In making major investments, an increasing number of internationally active enterprises consider control so critical that in those cases where they cannot obtain at least majority ownership they insist on an explicit agreement with the partner over certain key management decisions from the outset. They may seek partners who will be content to assume no management role or to confine their activities to certain limited areas. A number of these enterprises have come to insist on elaborate licensing arrangements and management contracts for their major new joint ventures. By these means, they seek to assure themselves greater freedom and flexibility in their management, but they are interested in making financial returns commensurate with their commitment of resources.

The dominance of joint ventures has been one of the noteworthy features of Japanese manufacturing investment abroad. The detailed analysis of Japanese practices reveals that such a preference is not an accidental phenomenon. Japanese firms tolerated or even preferred joint ventures because such partnerships were consistent with the firms' strategy and their relative lack of resources and international experience. Though the data are still quite sketchy, the available evidence does suggest that as Japan's emerging multinational enterprises seek new strategies and gain greater competence and resources, they are also likely, as a result, to pursue different ownership policies.

Table 5-1. Percentage of the value of materials and components purchased from parent companies by local subsidiaries of 50 Japanese manufacturing enterprises, by industry

INDUSTRY	PERCENTAGE OF INTERMEDIATE MATERIALS AND/OR COMPONENTS PURCHASED FROM THE PARENT COMPANY
Precision machinery	78.7
Transportation	75.8
Electric machinery	59.7
Ferrous and nonferrous metals	59.4
Chemicals	57.0
Nonelectrical machinery	47.5
Textiles	38.7
Paper and pulp	8.8

Source: Company records.

Table 5-2. Percentage of the output of foreign subsidiaries of 50 manufacturing enterprises sold in the local market

PERCENTAGE OF TOTAL DOMESTIC OUTPUT SOLD TO THE MARKET	NUMBER OF SUBSIDIARIES FALLING IN EACH OF THE CATEGORIES	PERCENTAGE
90 percent or more	304	72.9
50 percent or more but less than 90 percent	63	15.1
Less than 50 percent	50	12.0
	417	100.0

Source: Company records.

Table 5-3. Managers' assessments of the contributions of local partners in joint ventures, by stage of development of international business [a]

	AVERAGE RATING				NORMALIZED RATING		
CONTRIBUTION	TOTAL	EARLY	MODERATE	ACTIVE	EARLY	MODERATE	ACTIVE
Number of firms	87	22	42	23			
General knowledge of local environment	4.53	4.52	5.32	3.26	1.08	1.13	0.96
Government relations	4.41	4.83	4.79	3.20	1.36	1.63	0.80
General management	4.28	4.67	4.82	2.96	1.28	1.57	0.39
Labor relations	3.93	4.23	3.94	3.52	0.91	1.16	0.10
Access to local market	3.21	3.77	2.97	2.83	−0.05	−0.15	−0.45
Marketing policy	2.41	2.27	2.74	2.13	0.91	−1.16	−0.10
Access to raw materials	2.07	2.80	2.03	1.17	−0.62	−1.26	−1.36
Technology and manufacturing know-how	1.09	1.07	1.29	0.83	−2.34	1.92	−1.05

[a] Early means firms with five foreign manufacturing subsidiaries or fewer; moderate means firms with 6 to 14 foreign manufacturing subsidiaries; active means firms with 15 or more foreign manufacturing subsidiaries.

Table 5-4. Managers' assessments of the conflicts associated with local partners in joint ventures, by stages of international development [a]

| AREA OF CONFLICT | AVERAGE RATING | | | | NORMALIZED RATING | | |
	TOTAL	EARLY	MODERATE	ACTIVE	EARLY	MODERATE	ACTIVE
Transfer price	3.02	3.92	2.79	2.48	2.34	0.71	0.21
Disposition of earnings	2.59	2.13	2.97	2.61	0.60	0.88	0.37
Marketing	2.28	1.17	2.38	3.57	−0.34	0.41	1.32
Selection of products	2.15	1.47	2.09	3.13	−0.70	−0.07	0.95
Quality of products	2.08	1.73	1.94	2.74	0.20	−0.12	0.45
Pricing of the output	2.01	1.70	2.29	1.96	−0.42	0.27	−0.29
Selection of Japanese executives	1.94	1.37	2.35	2.05	0.11	0.48	−0.4
Use of Japanese manu- facturer's brand	1.74	1.00	2.09	2.17	0.20	0.20	0.25
Expansion	1.57	1.37	1.85	1.87	1.40	−0.12	−0.98
Payment of royalties and fees	1.02	0.57	1.85	1.87	−0.92	−1.18	−0.55
Export	0.91	0.53	0.79	1.52	−1.08	−1.24	−0.73

[a] Early means firms with five foreign manufacturing subsidiaries or fewer; moderate means firms with six to fourteen foreign manufacturing subsidiaries; active means firms with fifteen or more foreign subsidiaries.

Table 5-5. Major manufacturing investments made since 1970 in which the parent company has either majority or 100 percent control

COMPANY	COUNTRY	YEAR	PERCENT CONTROL	PRODUCT	METHOD OF ENTRY	MARKET
Matsushita	United States	1974	100	Color television	–	Local
Matsushita	Malaysia	1973	100	Electronic parts	New	Export
Matsushita	Spain	1973	80	TV, radio, air-conditioners, and tape recorders	–	Local
Matsushita	Great Britain	1974	100	Television sets	New	Local
Sanyo Electric	Korea	1973	100	Integrated circuits	New	Export
Sony	England	1974	100	Color television	New	Local and export
Sony	Brazil	1973	100	Color television	New	Local and export
Sony	United States	1972	100	Color television	New	Local
Toshiba	Korea	1970	70	Electronic parts	–	Export
Toshiba	Malaysia	1973	100	Electronic parts	New	Export
Toshiba	Brazil	1973	100	Electronic parts	Acquisition	Local
Hitachi	Malaysia	1972	90	Electronic parts	New	Export
Teijin	Indonesia	1973 1971	80	Polyester staples and filament	New	Export
Toray	Indonesia	1971	70	Nylon filament	New	Local
Nihon Denki	Brazil	1970	100	Telephone equipment	New	Local
Nihon Denki	Australia	1970	100	Telecommunications equipment	New	Local
Mitsubishi Heavy Industries	Brazil	1973	100	Machineries	New	Local
Kawasaki Heavy Industries	United States	1973	100	Motorcycles	New	Local

Source: Company records.

6. The Managerial System

We have seen that in organizational structure and ownership policies Japanese multinational enterprises have begun to manifest signs of convergence toward the pattern established by United States firms. One aspect of Japanese multinational enterprises yet to be examined is the managerial system. Here, the Japanese and American systems differ in some fundamental ways.

It has been well demonstrated that in expanding on a multinational level, U.S. enterprises drew on their strength in advanced technologies and on marketing skills first acquired in the high-income large market. Although the effects cannot be precisely measured, the system of management which evolved in large American enterprises at home also facilitated their multinational spread. Alfred Chandler has demonstrated that large American enterprises developed a distinct system of management as they pursued both geographic and product diversification. The sheer size of the domestic market alone necessitated a high degree of decentralization and a formal system of control. It is not unreasonable to assume that the management system thus developed aided a great deal in the multinational spread of large American companies. For many such multinational enterprises, the creation and management of subsidiaries across the Atlantic did not represent much of a departure from their efforts to spread their activities across the United States. In fact, a number of enterprises sought expansion abroad and in the domestic market almost simultaneously.

In sharp contrast, Japan's distinctive managerial system, which was nurtured in the home environment and proved effective in that setting, is an important factor inhibiting the growth of Japanese multinational enterprise. Unlike the areas of strategy and

161

structure, there appears to be little likelihood of convergence with the American system in managerial practices. Before turning to an analysis of managerial systems in Japanese multinational enterprise, let us first briefly identify the salient features of the Japanese system and how they developed from the roots in Japanese society.

A striking characteristic of Japanese society is its homogeneity, a point invariably noted in discussions of Japan and one whose importance cannot be overemphasized. Confined to small islands with only limited opportunities for physical contact with the outside world for two thousand years or so, the Japanese developed as a single race sharing the same language and culture. There are few major ethnic groups in the history of the world that have been as isolated and insulated as the Japanese. The cultural homogeneity that was nurtured for so many centuries was further reinforced by a peculiar type of centralized feudal system established by the Tokugawa regime in the seventeenth century, which lasted for two and a half centuries until the Meiji Restoration of 1868.

Another well-recognized feature of traditional Japanese social structure is a strong group orientation. Historically, every aspect of life was intricately bound to a group—the family, the village, the state. The norms and standards of the group ruled the individual's thoughts and actions. The most important criterion for judging actions and behavior was whether they were best for the group.

The emphasis on collectivity has deep historical roots. Japanese society developed from small, localized farming communities. In such communities, families tended to perpetuate themselves unchanged for generations, even to the point where the entire settlement took on the characteristics of one large family.[1] In such a society, individuals soon come to be closely interrelated, forming an "exclusive social nexus." [2] Out of this developed a considerable degree of interdependence, not only among individuals within a family but also among families within the settlement. One's welfare was closely tied to the prosperity of the group as a whole. The individual was identified with the group to such an extent that whatever one did immediately and totally reflected on the collective organization.

The most important group was the family, which emerged as a collective organization of much broader significance than a purely biological kinship group. The family system came to serve as the model for structuring all types of secondary groups, including the largest and most extensive—the nation state.

Another noteworthy traditional feature of Japan was the heavy emphasis on hierarchy in defining interpersonal relationships within a group. An individual's status was defined clearly and meticulously according to a hierarchical scale cemented by a set of mutual obligations. Appropriate behavior was strictly prescribed for each person according to his station in life.

In Japan's efforts to industrialize, the country was remarkably effective in transplanting traditional social values of the feudal and agrarian environment to a modern industrial setting. Although the ruling elite which guided Japan's industrialization borrowed extensively from the institutional frameworks of the West, they carefully retained many of the traditional values. This fact is usually cited as a main reason for Japan's success in achieving rapid industrialization with a minimum of social disruption. With the rise of large enterprises in the late nineteenth century, Japanese industries developed a blend of Western bureaucratic structures and traditional social values which has remained effective throughout much of this century.

It is in this environment that Japan's managerial system evolved. One of the hallmarks of the system is the special relationship between individuals and the firm, especially in large enterprises. The tie between company and employees is permanent. With virtually no exceptions, an employee of large firms enters the corporation at the time of his graduation from school and stays with the organization for his entire career. This so-called permanent employment, though, is not based on a contract; instead the relationship between employee and company is governed by a sense of obligation and in many ways is far more binding and extensive than a legal arrangement. In return for an implicit guarantee of lifetime security, the organization demands almost total commitment from the employee—not only his technical or professional contribution but, more important, his emotional tie to the firm, the traditional basis of identification of the individual's welfare with that of the group.

It should be pointed out that Japanese corporate organization is also strongly hierarchical. The status of each person is precisely defined and his behavior carefully prescribed. Within the corporate organization, the group constitutes the basic unit of work. Tasks are assigned to a group; the individual's function within the group is defined vaguely, if at all. Although the individual's status is strictly taken into account in maintaining the legitimate order in interpersonal relationships, particularly when the group deals with outside elements, the role and functions of individual members for task performance are readily adjustable, depending on the nature of the task and other conditions. Thus, the rigidity with which one's rank in the corporate structure is defined is compensated for by a high degree of flexibility in the determination of one's role on the job. An individual in such a system enjoys considerable freedom, subject to three conditions: he must work within the overall direction set by the group; he must show appropriate deference toward those who are superior in status, even though they are sometimes clearly inferior to the particular individual in other respects, such as technical competence; he must not seek personal recognition for his contributions.

The individual's assignments are determined largely by the nature of the task and the competence and qualifications of the members of the group. For such a system to work effectively in a given situation, the group requires initiative and direction— generally conceived of as important prerequisites of leadership in the American system of management. A quality of prime importance for a leader in the Japanese context is his ability to increase the productivity of the group. A leader in the Japanese system is one who can distribute work effectively within the group according to the ability and experience of each member and who can give each member freedom of action and yet be able to maintain harmony within the organization. He must also be capable of protecting and promoting his group's interests in relation to other groups and external forces.

Another notable feature of the Japanese managerial system is its reward system. The most important criterion for determining rewards is seniority. Career progress is predictable, well paced, and strictly controlled. At least through middle management ranks, advancement is automatic and progress is orderly. One should not, however, conclude that ability and performance are ignored. This is certainly not the case; both are acknowledged and rewarded. The Japanese style of performance evaluation and reward, however, differs from the American practice in two important ways. The Japanese system is much less formal, and the time span for evaluation is much longer. One is watched constantly by superiors, peers, and even subordinates over a period of time, and the tangible manifestations of reward for outstanding performance occur only when there is a consensus that special recognition is deserved. Even then it is carefully controlled. In a group-oriented system, singling out one individual for outstanding performance prematurely not only threatens the productivity of a group as a whole but reduces or destroys the subsequent effectiveness of the individual.

Because an individual's functions are ambiguously defined, the distribution of work within a group is almost invariably inequitable. Those who are capable tend to become overworked. Financial reward, being largely pegged to seniority, offers little differentiation in the short run between those with an outstanding record of performance and those with limited ability. Instead, short-term compensation takes the form of recognition and respect from the leader and the group and the opportunity to exert greater influence in the organization than one's formal rank normally allows.

One of the most complex aspects of Japanese managerial practice is the decision-making process commonly followed in large bureaucratic organizations, the so-called Ringi system. The system is popularly described as an approval-seeking process in which the proposal, or *ringisho*, is prepared by a lower functionary, works itself up through the organizational hierarchy in a circuitous manner, often at a snail's pace, and at each step is examined by the proper officials, whose approval is indicated by the affixing of a seal. Eventually, in the process, a decision emerges. The collection of seals is, however, only a procedural aspect whereby the decision already reached is formally approved. The substance of the Ringi system is far more complicated.

Indeed, the Ringi system defies neat definition. It is a group-oriented, consensus-seeking process that could only operate in the climate of the traditional Japanese concept of organization. It is also intimately related to the strong emphasis which the Japanese have traditionally placed on implicit, unspoken understanding between individuals. One consequence of this attitude is an aversion to explicit definition of organizational goals and policies and a strong preference for dealing with each major decision on an ad hoc basis as the need arises. The Ringi system is group-oriented and consensus-seeking in the sense that various interest groups which may be affected by a decision, as well as those who must implement it, participate in making the decision. A final decision eventually takes shape as a result of these group interactions, rather than being made explicitly by an individual who occupies the formal leadership role. This consensus-building process is accomplished by informal means. Discussions, consultations, persuasion, bargaining, or even arm-twisting are all carried on through subtle, informal interpersonal contacts. From a very early stage during which a decision is being shaped, different ideas and various alternatives are explored, albeit informally. Different interests are accommodated, and compromises are sought. At the same time, the process of education, persuasion, and coordination among various groups takes place, a process commonly referred to as *nemawoshi*. In these negotiations, IOUs for support of future or past decisions are issued or collected. An implicit tally of mutual obligations incurred in the process is kept in minute detail for future use. The Ringi system, of course, has no formal control mechanism whereby the result of a particular decision is monitored and the result is measured. Instead, the system again relies on informal processes, and the eventual outcome of a decision becomes known to virtually everyone in the organization. Such knowledge doubtless plays an important part in subsequent proposals made by the particular group.

Those reared in the tradition of American corporate culture cannot help wondering how Japanese organizations maintain their vigor and productivity in the absence of a formal control mechanism and an explicit system of performance evaluation supported by immediate financial reward. The answer is that the Japanese corporation relies on—and consciously fosters—emotional commitment to the organization by employees at every level. Socialization to the corporate culture begins at recruitment and continues throughout an employee's career. The young men who are carefully selected among graduates of outstanding universities survive a series of rigorous screening processes and are already highly homogeneous in their ability, background, and values. From the very first day upon joining the company, they go through an intensive socialization process, during which they are indoctrinated with the value orientation of the firm. To elicit and maintain a high degree of emotional commitment to the organization, a variety of means is employed, including extensive involvement of the company in the personal affairs of the employees.

In an organization consisting of a close, permanent web of relationships, communication takes on a special meaning. There is less need for verbalization; things do not have to be spelled out. In the words of an old Japanese saying: *ishi denshin*—the heart understands the heart. Communication thus often takes nonverbal forms; one is expected to read the minds of others without resorting to verbal articulation. In fact, in a closed system where everyone is intimately acquainted with one another, one may be accused of insensitivity and naivete if he seeks clear articulation of someone else's point of view.

In going abroad, Japanese enterprise took with it its own managerial system. To research the managerial style of Japanese foreign subsidiaries, I undertook a detailed study of a sample of twenty-five Japanese subsidiaries in Thailand where they were engaged in a number of fields, including metal fabrication and the manufacture of synthetic fiber, home appliances, consumer electronics, automobiles, and chemicals and related products. The companies were selected on the basis of three criteria: they were among the largest in a given industry in terms of sales and investment; they had had at least three years of operating experience; and their Japanese parent company had an active role in management of the subsidiaries. The conclusions which emerged from the study were further verified by an examination of similar subsidiaries in Malaysia and Taiwan.

Japanese managers, raised in their peculiar home environment and unfamiliar with any other system, had, like their counterparts from other countries, sought to extend their own system abroad. But the very characteristics of the Japanese system caused some serious tensions.

One major source of tension was the presence of large numbers of Japanese in the subsidiaries. The heavy use of Japanese managers in the subsidiaries is evident from the following data. The number of Japanese managers in the 25 subsidiaries studied ranged from 9 to 34, with an average of 16. The numbers are significant in view of the limited size of the operations. There were only three firms in the sample which had more than one thousand employees.

As summarized in Table 6-1, with the exception of jobs relating to labor and personnel, Japanese managers tended to occupy almost all key positions. In addition, positions below these were often staffed by Japanese junior managers. In some cases, even first-line supervisory positions in the plants were held by Japanese. True, in developing countries such as Thailand, there is a scarcity of managerial and technical know-how which necessitates the frequent use of expatriate personnel. Yet in comparison with American and European subsidiaries, Japanese subsidiaries have far greater numbers of Japanese managers occupying key positions, even given the more recent origin of Japanese overseas investment.

An obvious reason for the heavy use of Japanese personnel in subsidiaries is the language barrier. Unlike English, Japanese is hardly a universal language, and few Japanese are fluent in foreign languages, since such training at schools is poor. The insular nature of the country means that the average Japanese manager is rarely exposed to situations where he must use English. Equally rare, of course, is the local national who has a command of the Japanese language and who also has experience or potential as a manager.

Another reason for heavy commitment of Japanese personnel is the dependence of a typical Japanese corporate organization on shared experience and understanding and on the individual employee's emotional commitment to the organization; an organizational entity with these values cannot be created without having a sufficient number of people who have been reared within the system. In effect, there is a need for critical mass in the number of Japanese managers at the subsidiaries if the system is to function. This point was succinctly noted by a Thai manager who had worked for both Japanese and American subsidiaries in his country. He pointed out that the first thing the Americans did was to translate their detailed operating manuals and handbooks of procedures into the local language for the benefit of local managers. The Japanese, on the other hand, imported a whole team of Japanese personnel to create the organization on the Japanese model.

The Japanese manager who must head the foreign subsidiary is so wedded to the traditional managerial system of his country that he would find it impossible to manage an organization without the support of subordinates who share the same work style. A typical person managing a Japanese subsidiary abroad has had at least twenty years of experience and has occupied a middle management position at the parent company. He is used to having ideas generated from below and to relying heavily on the consensus process of decision making.

Finally, there is a strong need for the subsidiary to interact with the parent company in the solicitation of support and resources. In almost any multinational enterprise, an important task of expatriate managers is to serve as a communications link between the parent company and the subsidiary. Because the Japanese organization is a closed one and places strong emphasis on shared understanding, the communications role is particularly important.

The relationship between the subsidiary and the parent company raises some difficult problems for Japanese enterprises. Problems associated with managing far-flung foreign subsidiaries have been studied in some detail for U.S. and European enterprises. A variety of factors such as physical, cultural, and psychological distance between expatriate management and those at the parent company and differing conditions in various countries complicates the relationship. My study suggests that in this area the traditional Japanese style of management presents particular difficulties.

In Japanese corporate systems, there exists a strong hierarchical relationship between the parent company and its subsidiaries. In terms of the Japanese concept of the family, a subsidiary is analogous to a branch family, one not of direct lineage and is therefore inferior to the main house. In the corporate organization, the subordinate position of a subsidiary is further reinforced by a pattern of personnel practices that is a telling reflection of the way subsidiaries are viewed. This pattern consists of using the subsidiaries as havens for managers who have reached the compulsory retirement age at the parent company or who are younger but of limited competence. The practice of offering lifetime employment, together with a seniority-based reward system, tends to encourage early retirement. In most Japanese corporations, retirement age is between fifty-five and sixty. Companies usually continue to assume responsibility for the personal welfare of their employees even after they retire. They are usually named to positions appropriate to their status in one of the company's subsidiaries. The permanent employment practice also makes it necessary to find appropriate assignments for those who do not fit into the parent company. They are often shifted to foreign subsidiaries, sometimes in mid-career, just as domestic subsidiaries have been known to be used for such a purpose.

The pressure of a strong hierarchical relationship often results in dominance over subsidiaries—both domestic and foreign—by the parent company. Thus, there is a tendency for the parent company to impose its will on the subsidiaries.

Another complication arises from the fact that because tasks are defined ambiguously, the manager of a subsidiary must have an intuitive understanding of which types of decision can be made by him and which must be referred to the parent company. One theoretical criterion is that if a matter requires any significant commitment of parent company resources, it must be decided by the parent company. In practice the question is infinitely more subtle. On certain matters, the parent company expects to be consulted, while on others, after-the-fact reporting will suffice. A new manager of a foreign subsidiary is often told by his superiors prior to his departure that he will have total freedom of action in managing the subsidiary. The statement is made with full understanding on the part of everyone that no major decisions will be made without appropriate consultation with the parent company. As typically occurs in domestic operations, consideration of a proposal almost always originates at the lower levels of the organization, in this case at the subsidiary level. The decision-making process that follows is expected to conform to the domestic pattern. This presents enormous difficulties for the subsidiary, primarily because one of the elements that makes the Ringi system work is missing—the physical proximity which allows frequent interpersonal contact. Subsidiary managers are seriously handicapped by their inability to engage in extended, informal, face-to-face discussion. Particularly difficult is the initial stage of exploration, during which views and reactions to a tentative proposal are elicited from relevant groups on an informal basis before the proposal is officially submitted. In many ways, this is the most critical stage, for this is the point when compromises are made and bargains are struck. Effective operation of the Ringi system also requires that the subsidiary managers appreciate the current climate of the parent company; they must be aware of competing demands originating from other departments which may have direct impact on a proposal made by the subsidiary. The manager of the subsidiary experiences considerable difficulty in determining how to structure and present a proposal so as to increase its chances of acceptance and, above all, to obtain implicit commitments of support from other groups.

Because informal coordination among everyone concerned is so vital in the process of decision making, the senior manager of a subsidiary must allocate a considerable amount of time for informal discussion and negotiations. When an important decision is to be made, he often finds that he must mobilize other Japanese managers to lobby for that decision. As the senior Japanese manager of a subsidiary begins his discussion with individuals and groups in the parent company, other expatriate managers, representing different functional areas and with their own personal ties, begin informal exploratory discussions of their own regarding aspects of the proposal for which each is responsible. Typically, all these men, having come from their respective departments in the parent company, still enjoy personal contacts at their home base, and they are in a position both to engage in informal educational efforts and to lobby for the project. Views informally solicited from the various units are reflected in the final proposal so as to assure their approval when the proposal is formally presented. Informal lobbying, negotiations, and discussions also help fill the informational gap as well as to create a sympathetic climate in each group for the decision under consideration prior to its formal presentation. These activities supplement in important ways the efforts made by senior management. Because of the ties binding those who have had common experiences and similar organizational affiliations, the personnel of various units in the parent company, whether they be in plant, product division, or staff department are likely to feel a sense of obligation and allegiance to those in the foreign subsidiary whom they consider their representatives. Thus, a plea for support coming from former colleagues assigned to the parent company is much more effective than a request routed from the international division or even from the head of the subsidiary. Since, in the Ringi system, every relevant department participates in the decision-making process, it is vital to build a sympathetic climate within every unit concerned with a given decision. This is one of the major reasons for requiring a large complement of Japanese personnel from the parent company in foreign subsidiaries. Only those with appropriate contacts and experience at the parent company could engage effectively in these subtle negotiations.

The heavy emphasis placed on personal ties makes foreign assignments unattractive to Japanese managers. Personal relations once built must be sustained by frequent contact to be effective; foreign assignments tend to erode these close relationships.

Chie Nakane, an authority on Japanese social structure, characterizes interpersonal relationships in a Japanese organization as tangible. Nakane notes that the social organization which causes an individual to be engrossed so deeply in personal relations at the same time that he is distant geographically limits the scope of his personal relations.[3] Nakane argues that such a highly localized and exclusive relationship also tends to produce particular relationships.[4] Group unity is maintained by strong emphasis on emotional commitment. An appeal to emotion, though most effective, requires constant face-to-face contact. Thus, whatever emotional commitment to himself a manager has been able to build up with his colleagues in the organization is his most important personal asset in the company. Of course, the asset is company specific and cannot be taken to another organization. The absence or the loss of tangibility from the main body for an extended period of time invariably means the erosion of this all-critical social asset.

An important aspect of building such assets is the availability of opportunities to demonstrate one's competence. As noted earlier, performance evaluation in Japanese companies is informal. One must build a record of performance over a period of time. To build such a reputation requires close working relationships with managers at different levels and with different functions. A reputation must be built among relevant groups at the center of the organization. One's record of performance at a remote subsidiary, however excellent, contributes little to the process.

The fact that a foreign assignment means almost invariably the erosion of the manager's social assets is a real deterrent to his assuming an assignment abroad. Career risks associated with foreign assignments are certainly not confined to Japanese managers. In fact, it is a major concern for managers working for many U.S. multinational enterprises. For Japanese multinational enterprises, however, the matter is more complicated for the reasons just noted. These considerations make internal recruitment of outstanding managers for foreign assignments extremely difficult. In the Japanese system, one does not refuse an assignment once it is made, but there are many ways, particularly for capable middle managers, to let one's reluctance be known and for all practical purposes to sabotage the assignment. Not infrequently, those sent abroad consider their assignment more or less an exile.

I observed in my field study that those who were assigned abroad expended a great deal of effort to keep up their contacts at the home office and thus to arrest any serious deterioration of personal relationships within relevant groups in the parent company. The renewal of personal ties was a central concern on trips to the parent company. The managers abroad devoted a considerable amount of time to private correspondence with former associates in order to keep abreast of the climate of the parent company, although fully recognizing that this was a poor substitute for regular face-to-face contacts.

In certain ways, the strong orientation toward the parent company is an asset to the Japanese multinational enterprise, for this is a powerful system of control. The organizational identification shared by Japanese managers facilitated the worldwide expansion of trading companies in the decade prior to World War II. Orientation toward the parent company in Japan means that the Japanese expatriate managers are not deeply concerned with building their ties with the local communities in which they operate. For trading companies, this did not pose a serious problem, since trading in basic commodities and cheap consumer nondurable goods did not require building lasting relationships with either customers or suppliers. But for subsidiaries engaged in manufacturing of capital intensive and technically oriented goods entailing strong local marketing efforts and resource requirements, the situation is quite different. They must build strong and enduring ties with consumers, dealers, suppliers, as well as with other elements of the local community. For these firms, the Japanese managers' preoccupation with maintaining their relationship with the parent company has become a major problem: how to maintain a balance between necessary local commitments and the parent company.

The most serious problem of the Japanese management system in the multinational setting is that it cannot effectively integrate local nationals into the mainstream of management in the foreign subsidiaries. True, most of the local employees among the companies studied were too young and inexperienced to have a major voice in management whatever the system, but even those who had substantial experience found it difficult to assert their influence in the subsidiary. The language barrier makes it difficult for foreign nationals to communicate effectively with the Japanese personnel, while Japanese expatriates generally have only a limited command of the local language. Thus the amount of communication between Japanese and local managers is limited.

Even more fundamental, of course, is the local employees'

lack of common membership in the parent company, and consequently the lack of shared understanding that unites its employees, for without such membership, one cannot become a full-fledged part of the system. The difference in nationality is less a barrier than the lack of proper corporate lineage, so to speak. Even Japanese nationals who are recruited locally by the subsidiary suffer from this handicap, where even their fluency in Japanese and their cultural heritage are not sufficient for them to be accepted as full-fledged members of the organization. Japanese employees recruited locally become, in effect, mere functionaries and interpreters, regardless of seniority or experience.

Despite the system's inability to accommodate and integrate those who lack common membership in the parent company, Japanese subsidiaries nonetheless follow personnel management policies similar to those designed for employees at home. As observed in the field study, Japanese subsidiaries generally prefer to recruit young men directly from college. Once recruited, these men begin their training and day-to-day activities at the bottom of the organization; they go through a socialization process similar to that experienced by Japanese junior managers. While the programs abroad tend to be less formal and sophisticated, the underlying philosophy remains the same.

The local employees, however, quickly recognize the inconsistency between personnel policies designed to develop managers thoroughly socialized into the system, and their own failure to achieve real integration. I managed, although with some difficulty, to obtain the views of local nationals of Thailand, Malaysia, and Taiwan employed by Japanese firms as management trainees. Some recognized certain benefits associated with employment in a Japanese firm. It does provide one with a decent job and a respectable salary, if not with a responsible assignment. Japanese reluctance to dismiss employees short of serious moral offense was considered advantageous, particularly in contrast to American companies which offer no such guarantee. A number of respondents also noted that the Japanese managers they worked for showed concern for their personal welfare and were anxious to offer assistance when personal problems arose.

Despite these favorable reactions, the major concern expressed by local nationals was, understandably, their inability to gain promotion to really responsible positions. They all noted how difficult it was to share in the exclusive social relationships maintained by Japanese expatriate personnel. Throughout the field study, these men almost invariably contrasted personnel procedure of American and Japanese multinational enterprises. They pointed to the fact that American subsidiaries were better prepared to accept local nationals for key management posts than were Japanese firms. They were quick to recognize that the difference was in part due to the stage of development of the companies in question; on the average, the Japanese subsidiary was newer and the parent company less experienced in international operations. Yet they felt that the difference was far more basic. Some observed rather pointedly that the branches or subsidiaries of Japanese trading companies with many years of local presence had still not integrated local nationals into key managerial posts.

Some local·employees, faced with this situation, resign themselves to being relegated to clerical or junior management positions for their entire careers and, typically, do not show initiative. Neither do they volunteer their views and may perform a minimum amount of work. They learn how to deal with superiors who will occupy key positions for a limited time only.

The more ambitious local employees try to exploit whatever training opportunities the Japanese subsidiaries have to offer. For example, a number of local trainees, particularly those with technical backgrounds, go to Japan for extensive training at the parent company for as long as a year. Men with such training are in great demand in the local job market. Shortly after the trainees return home, many are lured away to more attractive positions with local firms or to more responsible positions with subsidiaries of other foreign companies. This behavior of local nationals is especially disturbing to Japanese managers, who expect the same degree of loyalty to the company from local nationals as they do from their Japanese employees. Such behavior on the part of local employees tends to color the Japanese managers' view of them, and the resulting negative attitude toward local nationals contributes further to the alienation of this group. Moreover, Japanese reluctance to promote local employees to responsible positions has become widely known, and Japanese firms have begun to experience difficulties in attracting outstanding nationals.

The inability of the Japanese system to allow for the promotion of local nationals to key management ranks will likely constrain the growth of Japanese multinational enterprises in two important ways. First, if the present practice of staffing subsidiaries with Japanese executives continues, it will place an enormous strain on the limited pool of Japanese managers qualified for foreign assignments. Even among the largest Japanese companies, particularly manufacturing enterprises, the number of Japanese managers who can function effectively abroad is limited. The second factor is cost. With rapidly increasing wage levels in Japan, the cost of supporting expatriate managers has become very high through allowances of various sorts. The total cost of maintaining a manager abroad is estimated to be at least double the level of his salary and fringe benefits at home. This has become a considerable burden to the small subsidiaries which dominate Japanese investments.

Moreover, the heavy use of Japanese managers is a source of concern to local partners in joint ventures. Indeed, the closed and exclusive managerial system has aroused serious resentment against Japanese multinational enterprises on the part of partners, customers, and government officials in host countries. Despite the limited presence of Japanese multinational enterprises in a number of countries, even here they have already come under severe attack. Although the manner of personnel assignment is not the sole target, it is almost always a major issue. In many countries, the heavy use of Japanese personnel in subsidiaries resulted in restrictions on the number of Japanese to be assigned to a given subsidiary. This is particularly troublesome to the Japanese because they have encountered pressure toward localization of management in multinational enterprises just as they were beginning to pursue a strategy emphasizing greater coordination among the subsidiaries.

Faced with these challenges, a handful of internationally active Japanese enterprises have begun to take a few positive steps. One is an attempt to formalize management responsibilities by introducing a semblance of standard operating procedure. Early attempts have not been sufficiently successful, however, as illustrated by the following example.

The international division of one of the most progressive Japanese multinational enterprises sought to define certain kinds of decisions which the manager of a subsidiary could make without consulting headquarters. If an investment decision involved less than a certain sum, the manager was free to act on his own. The system had been promoted by junior staff members in an effort to rationalize ambiguous decision-making practices, but to their frustration, the new system was practically ignored. When I inquired what impact an attempt to establish a standard operating procedure in this area had had on dealings with headquarters, the manager of the subsidiary in Thailand, one of the oldest and largest in this company, replied, "None whatsoever." Not only was he unable to recall his spending authorities, for example, but his assistant had some difficulty in locating the document itself.

Another measure that has been undertaken has been to make concentrated efforts to train Japanese managers specifically for foreign assignments. The content of the program varies and includes such elements as foreign language training and even sending select groups of young men to leading business schools for up to two years of graduate training.

Another step is that a few firms have begun to establish specific goals for the promotion of local nationals to key managerial positions in the face of pressure to assign larger numbers of them to responsible posts in the subsidiaries. These firms, of course, are very much aware of the kinds of problems noted earlier, which tend to reduce the effectiveness of the local managers, particularly in dealing with the parent company. To remedy this situation, some firms have tried to strengthen the international division by staffing area organizations with Japanese executives who have had some operating experience at the subsidiary level and who are both knowledgeable about the country and familiar with the local managers themselves. In effect, these managers in the international division become intermediaries on behalf of the subsidiaries in dealing with various staff groups at the parent company.

All these steps are designed to increase organizational capacity to accommodate men with different cultural heritages. Particular emphasis has been placed so far on the development of a small core of men who could serve as the intermediary or buffer between the subsidiary and its local managers and the parent company. The question remains, however: can the Japanese management system adapt itself to accommodate heterogeneous elements and still function effectively in the international marketplace?

The Japanese have done well to adapt, on a selective basis, concepts, institutions, and technology foreign to the Japanese setting; they have done so with a minimum of social disruption. Their achievements in this regard during the past century have been remarkable and have been credited as a major factor in

Japan's rapid modernization and industrialization. Those familiar with Japanese practices in this regard are aware that the process goes far beyond mere imitation.

Japanese management faces a serious dilemma. In order to undertake major expansion internationally, the Japanese must bring about basic changes in their management system— changes that will not be easy to achieve. And in the process, they may well sacrifice those elements that have made their system so effective internally. The optimist would cite the remarkable Japanese ability to achieve what appears to be all but impossible through ingenuity and diligence, and he would also point to the great success the Japanese have achieved in assimilating foreign institutions and technology. Clearly, however, what is demanded now of Japanese management is fundamentally different from the adoption of certain elements of foreign culture into their tightly knit and homogeneous cultural setting. The past offers no assurance in this regard, and the outcome is by no means certain.

Table 6-1. Extent to which Japanese managers held key positions in 25 Japanese manufacturing subsidiaries in Thailand, 1973

POSITION	PERCENTAGE OF JAPANESE MANAGERS
Chairman of the board	31.5
President	56.5
Executive vice-president	61.2
Accounting manager	87.0
Production manager	85.6
Marketing manager	80.2
Personnel manager	51.3
General affairs manager	61.7

Source: Field survey.

Notes

1. The Setting

1. Alfred D. Chandler, Jr., *Strategy and Structure: Chapters on the History of the American Industrial Enterprise* (Cambridge, Mass.: MIT Press, 1962). Chandler defines strategy as "the determination of the basic long-term goals and objectives of an enterprise, and the adoption of courses of action and allocation of resources necessary for carrying out these goals." He goes on to note that the crucial elements of strategy are the volume of activities, geographical expansion, research, and product diversification (p. 13). Structure, according to Chandler, is "the design of organization through which the enterprise is administered. It includes, first, the line of authority and communications between the different administrative offices and officers and, second, the information and data that flow through these lines of communication and authority" (p. 14).

2. For an excellent analysis of this period see Edwin O. Reischauer, *The United States and Japan* (Cambridge, Mass.: Harvard University Press, 1965), pp. 51–120.

3. William W. Lockwood, *Economic Development of Japan* (Princeton, N.J.: Princeton University Press, 1953), pp. 5–68.

4. Thomas C. Smith, *Political Changes and Industrial Development in Japan* (Stanford, Calif.: Stanford University Press, 1955), pp. 10–58.

5. Ibid., pp. 105–117.

6. For further discussion of the Meiji ideology see my *Japan's Managerial System* (Cambridge, Mass.: MIT Press, 1968), pp. 48–84.

7. For a detailed discussion of Zaibatsu see Lockwood, *Economic Development of Japan*, pp. 204–284. Eleanor O. M. Hadley, *Antitrust in Japan* (Princeton, N.J.: Princeton University, 1970), pp. 20–32.

8. R. P. Dore, *City Life in Japan: A Study of Tokyo Ward* (Berkeley, Calif.: University of California Press, 1958), pp. 262–268. See also Takeyashi Kawashima, *Ideology toshite no kazokuseido* (The family system as an ideology; Tokyo: Iwanami Shoten, 1964), pp. 6–175.

9. See my *Japan's Managerial System*, pp. 162–195.

10. For an analysis of business and government interactions in postwar Japan see Eugene J. Kaplan, *Japan's Government-Business Relationship* (Washington, D.C.: U.S. Department of Commerce, 1972), pp. 5–90.

11. *Kagaku gitsu yoran, 1972* (A summary of statistics of science and technology, 1972; Tokyo: Kagaku Gitsu Cho 1973), p. 121.

12. On the restructuring of postwar Zaibatsu and emergence of bank-centered groups see my *Japan's Managerial System*, pp. 118–134.

13. *Rodo hakusho, 1973* (White paper on labor, 1973; Tokyo: Ministry of Labor, 1973).

14. *Ka kyo hakusho* (White paper on the environment; Tokyo: The Environmental Agency, 1972), p. 9.

15. For example, from February through May of 1974, sales of Japanese automobiles in the United States showed a rather drastic decline compared with the same period in 1973. In May 1974 sales were off 38 percent from May of the previous year. Wage increases and revaluations resulted in a price differential of as much as $1,000 between comparable Japanese and American automobiles.

16. As late as 1969 the accumulated total of foreign direct investment was no more than $482 million.

17. Of the $1,660 million invested in Europe, $1,410 million, or nearly 85 percent was invested in Great Britain. Approximately 93 percent of it is accounted for by two types of investment—loans extended to British shipping companies by Japanese shipbuilders in connection with the sales of ships and the recent partial acquisition of a subsidiary of the British Petroleum Company located in Abu Dhabi, amounting to $780 million. This is the single largest private foreign investment by Japanese companies.

2. Ventures in Raw Materials

1. For an excellent description of pattern development of the Japanese petroleum industry see Long Term Credit Bank of Japan, *Shuyo sangyo sengo nijugonen shi* (A twenty-five year history of major Japanese industries; Tokyo: Sangyo to Keizai, 1972), pp. 57–60.

2. *Sekyu tokei shiryo, 1973* (Statistics on the petroleum industry, 1973; Tokyo: The Ministry of International Trade and Industry, 1974), p. 18.

3. Ibid., p. 10.

4. For the analysis of Japanese managerial ideology see my *Japan's Managerial System*, pp. 48–117.

5. The "coming of the black ships" refers to the visit of Commodore Matthew Perry's fleet of gunboats to the Tokyo Bay in 1853, which was considered a major national threat and provided a major impetus for the overthrow of the Tokugawa feudal system.

6. For details see my "Japan as a Host to International Corporations"

in Charles Kindleberger, ed., *The International Corporation* (Cambridge, Mass.: MIT Press, 1971), pp. 142–161.

7. For an excellent study of competitive matching behavior in oligopolistic industries see Frederick T. Knickerbocker, *Oligopolistic Reaction and Multinational Enterprises* (Boston, Mass.: Division of Research, Harvard Business School, 1973).

8. Raymond Vernon, *Sovereignty at Bay* (New York, N.Y.: Basic Books, Inc., 1971), pp. 33–37.

9. For details see Edith T. Penrose, *The Large International Firm in Developing Countries: The International Petroleum Industry* (Cambridge, Mass.: MIT Press, 1968), pp. 150–172.

10. Vernon, *Sovereignty at Bay*, pp. 29–30.

11. Ibid. See also Penrose, *The Large International Firm*, pp. 29–51.

12. Vernon, *Sovereignty at Bay*, pp. 30–31.

13. For details see Penrose, *The Large International Firm*, pp. 97–148.

14. Ibid., p. 148.

3. The Spread of Manufacturing

1. Raymond Vernon, *Sovereignty at Bay* (New York, N.Y.: Basic Books, Inc., 1971), pp. 13–18.

2. The following analysis on the evolution of U.S. multinational enterprises on the manufacturing industries draws heavily from Vernon, *Sovereignty at Bay*, pp. 65–87.

3. See my *Japanese Marketing System* (Cambridge, Mass.: MIT Press, 1971), pp. 15–28.

4. Shuji Ohashi, *Tekkogyo* (The steel industry; Tokyo: Toyo Neizai, 1971), pp. 197–297.

5. Hoshimi Uchida, *Gosei sehi kogyo* (The synthetic fiber industry; Tokyo: Toyo Keizai, 1971), pp. 161–246.

6. Ryotaro Koyama, "Katei denki" (Home appliances), in H. Kumagai, ed., *Nihon no sangyo soshiki* (Industrial organization in Japan; Tokyo: Chuo Koron Sha, 1973), pp. 15–82.

7. Japan Long Term Credit Bank, ed., *Shuyo sangyo sengo nijugonen shi* (A twenty-five year history of major Japanese industries; Tokyo: Sangyo to Keizai, 1972), pp. 421–472.

8. For a similar pattern observed among U.S. multinational enterprises, see Frederick Knickerbocker, *Oligopolistic Reaction and Multinational Enterprises*, pp. 53–84.

9. *Showa 47 nendo wagakuni kigyo no kaigai jigyo katsudo* (A survey of foreign activities of Japanese enterprises, fiscal year 1974; Tokyo: The Ministry of International Trade and Industry, 1973), p. 27.

10. Raymond Vernon, "The Location of Economic Activity," working paper, Harvard Business School, pp. 18–20.

11. For an account of similar developments in the automobile industry in Europe see Louis T. Wells, "Automobiles," in Raymond Ver-

non, ed., *Big Business and the State: Changing Relations in Western Europe* (Cambridge, Mass.: Harvard University Press, 1974), pp. 245–251.

12. Ibid., pp. 25–27.

13. For details see Richard D. Moxon, "Offshore Production in the Less-Developed Countries by American Electronics Companies," D.B.A. diss., Harvard Business School, June 1973.

14. "Production Costs of Radios and Television Sets Are Destined to Surpass Those of the U.S.," *Japan Economic Journal* (May 14, 1974), p. 8.

15. Masao Baba, "Bearing," in H. Kumaga, ed., *Nihon no sangyo soshiki* (Industrial organization in Japan; Tokyo: Chuo Koron Sha, 1971), pp. 325–346.

16. Vernon, *Sovereignty at Bay*, p. 111.

17. For an excellent analysis of multinational spread of the U.S. petrochemical industry see Robert B. Stobaugh, "The Product Life Cycle, U.S. Exports, and International Investment," D.B.A. diss., Harvard Business School, June 1968.

18. For example, see *Kagaku Gitsu Hakosho: Showa 49 Nendo* (White paper on science and technology, 1974; Tokyo: Ministry of International Trade and Industry, 1974), pp. 71–145. See also Industrial Bank of Japan, *Shichijunendai no Nihon sangyo* (Japanese industries in the 1970s; Tokyo: Nihon Keizai Shinbunsha, 1972), pp. 156–159.

19. Ibid.

20. Edwin Mansfield, *The Economies of Technological Change* (New York, N.Y.: McGraw-Hill, 1968), pp. 80–98. See also Vernon, *Sovereignty at Bay*, pp. 90–96.

5. The Manufacturing Firm

1. Sidney M. Robbins and Robert B. Stobaugh, *Money in the Multinational Enterprise* (New York, N.Y.: Basic Books, Inc., 1973), pp. 37–47.

2. Lawrence G. Franko, *Joint Venture Survival in Multinational Corporation* (New York, N.Y.: Praeger, 1971), pp. 81–141.

6. The Managerial System

1. Hajime Nakamura, *Ways of Thinking of Eastern Peoples: India, China, Tibet, Japan* (Honolulu: East-West Center Press, 1964), p. 413.

2. Ibid., pp. 413–414.

3. Chie Nakane, *Japanese Society* (Berkeley, Calif.: University of California Press, 1972), pp. 130–132.

4. Ibid.

Index

Advanced countries: restrictions against imports in, 20; Japanese defense of market position in, 77-80; investment in, 80

Advertising, increase in, 73

Africa: Japanese overseas investment in, 26; oil exploration in, 45

Air-conditioning units, manufacture of, 71, 73

Allied Occupation: effect on Zaibatsu, 10, 14; ban on oil refineries by, 36

Aluminum: Showa Denko, 15; Japanese import of, 25; involvement of trading companies in, 114; vertical integration in, 116

Amakadori, 54

American Metal Climax, 115

AMOCO, Singapore refinery, 51

Anglo-Persian Oil Co., 42

Arabian Oil Company, 39-40, 41; expansion of, 51, 52

Associated Oil, 35

Australia, 77, 115-116

Authoritarianism, in Zaibatsu, 6

Automobile industry: Nissan, 15; development of, 63, 64-65; international cooperation in, 77; expansion of, 89

Ball-bearings, 89; Japanese manufacture of within U.S., 81

Bank-centered groups, 15; attitude toward oil, 40-41; in consolidation of oil exploration, 47; vertical integration in, 50; in petrochemicals, 86

Banks, Japanese, international expansion of, 120

Bauxite, 115-116

Brand name, use of, 82, 90, 153

Brazil, 77; petrochemicals in, 86

British Petroleum, 51, 52, 53; in the oil crisis, 56; government role in, 57-58

Bureaucracy, and *Amakadori,* 54

Business leaders, Japanese, role of, 13-14. *See also* Leadership; Management

Caltex, 36, 51, 52; in the oil crisis, 56

Canada, photochemical complex in, 85

Capital liberalization, 43; and increase in imports, 24

Capital requirements, increase in, 140

Capolactum, 74

Celanese, 71

Ceylon, 116

Chandler, Alfred D., Jr., 2, 161

Chemicals: Showa Denko, 15; gain in importance of, 17, 63; difficulties of expansion in, 21-22. *See also* Petrochemical industry

City banks: financing of Zaikai firms by, 15; competition among, 16. *See also* Bank-centered groups

Coal, 10; importance of vs. oil, 35; dominance of, 36-37; shift from, 44

Coca Cola, 62

Collectivity, importance of, 6, 16. *See also* Groups

Communication: between parent company and subsidiary, 168-169; for decision-making, 170; between Japanese and local managers, 173

Compagnie Française des Pétroles, 42 56, 57-58